DIALOGUES ON MADNESS AND WISDOM

IN CONVERSATION WITH R.D. LAING

Vincenzo Caretti

Edited by Miles Groth & Danilo Serra

SEA
The Society for Existential Analysis
London

© First published 2022 by The Society for Existential Analysis

Typeset by Dean Andrews

All rights reserved. No part of this book may be reprinted or reproduced or utilised in any form or by any electronic, mechanical or other means, now known or hereafter invented, including photocopying and recording, or in any information storage or retrieval system, without permission in writing from the publishers.

British Library Cataloguing in Publishing Data
A catalogue record for this book is available from the British Library

ISBN 9798406565353

CONTENTS

Editor's Introductory Note iii
Translator's Introducton v
Preface to the English translation (2021) ix

DIALOGUE 1
From Bible to Zen 1

DIALOGUE 2
The Method of Science and the New Psychology 9

DIALOGUE 3
With Freud and After Freud... 20

DIALOGUE 4
...Jung 31

DIALOGUE 5
The Fate of the Family 35

DIALOGUE 6
Family and Schizophrenia 42

DIALOGUE 7
Between 'Journey' And Madness 52

DIALOGUE 8
Language, Time, Silence 61

DIALOGUE 9
On the Part of Young People and Women 66

DIALOGUE 10
Intellectual Work 75

DIALOGUE 11
A Profession of Faith 78

Endnotes 82

EDITOR'S INTRODUCTORY NOTE

While preparing Gion Condrau's *Martin Heidegger's Impact on Psychotherapy* (New York: Edition Mosaic, 1998) for a new edition (London: Free Associations Books, 2021), I decided to have a look at a book Condrau references in his chapter on 'The Role of Dreams in Daseinsanalysis', which was first published in 1991 in the journal *Psychoanalysis and Psychotherapy*. Published by Vincenzo Caretti as *Intervista sul Folle e il Saggio: Ronald D. Laing* (Rome: Laterza, 1979), the book is the text of interviews between Caretti and Laing which took place over a period of a week in London in 1978. It had been translated into Dutch (1980), Spanish (1980), German (1981) and Portuguese (1981) – but not into English, the language in which the interviews were originally conducted. Giovanni Ferrara had translated a transcription of the taped conversations between Laing, who was then fifty-one, and Caretti, then a young student of just twenty-five years of age. I was able to locate a copy of the book and saw that it was a treasure unknown to English-speaking readers.

By the time they met, Laing had published his major works *The Divided Self* (1960); *The Self and Others* (1961; rev. ed. 1969); *Reason and Violence* (1964, with David Cooper); *Sanity, Madness and the Family* (1964); *Interpersonal Perception* (1966, with Herbert Phillipson & A. Russell Lee); *The Politics of Experience and The Bird of Paradise* (1967); *The Politics of the Family and Other Essays* (1969); *Knots* (1970); *The Facts of Life* (1976); and *Conversations with Adam and Natasha* (1977), as well as numerous papers, lectures and book reviews. A few years later I attended a memorable lecture by Laing at the Society for Ethical Culture in New York. The venue was crowded and, to my regret, I missed an opportunity to meet him. In 1985, he was featured at the legendary 'Lourdes of Psychotherapy' attended by all of the great living psychotherapists of the time and he published his autobiographical study *Wisdom, Madness and Folly: The Making of a Psychiatrist*. Laing died only four years later, in 1989, a few months before his sixty-second birthday.

By chance, in late 2020, I had made the acquaintance of then doctoral candidate at the University of Bergamo, Danilo Serra, who had published a remarkable book *La Follia di Gesù [The Madness of Jesus]* (Naples: LFA Publisher, 2017). Our common interest was the philosophy of Martin Heidegger, about whom Danilo had written a book *Che cosa significa pensare in Heidegger. Per un'etica del pensare [What Does Thinking Mean in Heidegger: Toward an Ethic of Thinking]* the year before (Saonaro: Il Prato, 2016). Danilo had also contributed to a meeting of the Heidegger-Archive in Seville, directed by Alfred Denker, who may be thanked for the chance but timely encounter between Danilo and me.

The year 2020 was the first of COVID and we were all isolated: I was in New York, Danilo was in Agrigento. Danilo and I wrote to each other for several months about Heidegger and on one occasion I brought up the name Laing, which was somewhat new to the young scholar who was then only twenty-eight years old. My own work on daseinsanalysis, which is the topic of Condrau's book, included tracing Heidegger's influence on Laing, which Condrau had mentioned. This was confirmed by what we found in Caretti's book. Danilo and I contacted Caretti in Rome and he was delighted to hear of our idea of translating his Laing book, for which he held the rights. He granted them to us and over a period of six months, Danilo would translate several pages of the Italian text and send them to me. They were near-flawless English. On occasion, a term would come up that needed our collaboration on context. Sometimes it was an idiom that had to be captured with *la mot juste*. Given my rudimentary familiarity with Italian, the reader must understand that what follows is entirely the accomplishment of Danilo Serra. Professor Caretti read the translation, was delighted, and kindly agreed to write a Preface for this book.

In introducing these conversations, which are the fourth in a series of dialogues published by the Society for Existential Analysis, I feel gratified recalling that although "it was the worst of times", it was also "the best of times". I am pleased to have been able to play a part in bringing Caretti's work to the English-speaking reader. The world needs to be reminded of the accomplishment of the remarkable scholar and therapeut, R.D. Laing, especially at this juncture in history. My thanks go my young friend, now Dr. Danilo Serra; to Professor Vincenzo Caretti, whom it has been a delight to come to know; and to Paola Pomponi, the present Chair of the SEA and promoter of the SEA *Dialogues* series in which this book appears, who welcomed our contribution.

Miles Groth, PhD
New York, October 2021

TRANSLATOR'S INTRODUCTON
The Need to Read Laing Again.
On the Importance of Madness and Wisdom

Take music, sound and silence. In his Notebook for Anna Magdalena Bach, Bach wrote pieces of music that any young boy beginning to learn the piano can easily play. In two or three pages he explains the core of his musical theory, highlighting how in his music (which is contrapuntal music) the elements that constitute its form and meaning are not the notes but the relationships between the notes. It is the ratio of an octave followed by the ratio of a sixth, followed by the ratio of a third, followed by the ratio of a fifth...

Listening to Bach, or any other music, you start by hearing the notes. But if you transpose a melody, whistling or humming it (which more or less we all know how to do) to a different key, it becomes evident, even if you may not be fully aware of it, that what you are reacting to and translating in your own way is the relationship between the notes and not the notes themselves. Now, the relationship between notes is not a note. Indeed, this relation is not a sound, but the relation between two sounds. And what is the opposite of sound? Obviously silence. The fact is, then, that notes create a shimmering illusion, shaping silence into different textures or modules. What counts in the end is the interval between the notes, that is, the silence. It makes no noise, but it is what we hear, what we grasp as an octave, or as a perfect fifth.

(R.D. Laing, Madness and Wisdom: In Conversation with R.D. Laing)

In 1979, Jungian psychoanalyst Vincenzo Caretti published his account of discussions in London on a variety of topics with the Scottish existential psychiatrist and psychotherapist, Ronald David Laing (1927-1989): *Intervista sul folle e il saggio* (Rome: Laterza). Under Caretti's editorial supervision, the Italian text was prepared by Giovanni Ferrara. It was promptly translated into Dutch (*Over waanzin en wijsheid: Interview door Vincenzo Caretti*. Amsterdam: Wetenschappelijke Uitgeverij, 1980); Spanish (*Los locos y los cuerdos: Entrevista de Vincenzo Caretti*. Barcelona: Grupo Editorial Grijalbo, 1980); German (*Es stört mich nicht ein Mensch zu sein: Ein Gespräch mit Vincenzo Caretti*. Köln: Kiepenheuer & Witsch, 1981); and Portuguese (*Sobre loucos e sãos: Entrevista a Vincenzo Caretti*. São Paulo: Editora Brasiliense, 1981).

More than forty years have passed since the work first appeared. Now with the blessings of Professor Caretti and the great help and support of Professor Miles Groth, I have translated Caretti's important interview to Laing into English. The title of the book chosen for the English version (*Madness and Wisdom: In Conversation with R.D. Laing*) follows almost literally the original Italian one. *'Folle'* and *'saggio'*, as they are understood in the course of the pages of the text, are two words that we can render in English with 'madman' and 'wise man'. The second part of the title is an addition to the Italian version: first of all, it is intended to highlight the fact that the text is the fruit of an interview and thus of a conversation with Laing. Secondly, the sentence *In Conversation with R.D. Laing* is also intended to express the most radical and authentic sense of this book, which is that of a rethinking of Laing's thought. In fact, these conversations are a sort of narrative, an analysis of Laing's work through his professional and private life. It is not, therefore, simply a series of interviews, of which Laing gave many, but a priceless treasure trove through which we can read and understand all the influences, inspirations and impulses that contributed to the formation of the great Scottish psychiatrist.

The work has long been out of print but its striking contemporaneity compels, making it available to a new generation of scholars, psychotherapists and psychiatrists. Its importance may be judged by the similarity of the period in which Laing worked and exerted his greatest impact (1960-1985) to current events marked by worldwide political tensions, questions about the integrity of the family unit, the place of drugs in the treatment of psychological disorders and a return of interest in the interface between natural science and existential authenticity.

In conversing with his pupil, Caretti, and answering his questions, Laing expounds most of the basic themes of his own thought, including his critique of the concept of 'objectivity', the question about the meaning of the human condition and *the need to consider the mystery of the origin of experience*. For this reason the text translated here for the first time may be useful to better understand certain nuances of Laing's language and thought. It may also be useful to understand the special dialogue between Laing and all of us who encounter his thought, an ongoing, endless dialogue that revolves around the unsolvable problem of human experience, its "enigma" and "inaccessible abyss".

A review of the book's eleven chapter headings suggests the range of topics Caretti and Laing cover:

1. From the Bible to Zen
2. The Method of Science and the New Psychology
3. With Freud and After Freud …
4. … Jung
5. The Fate of the Family
6. Family and Schizophrenia
7. Between 'Journey' and Madness
8. Language, Time, Silence
9. On the Part of Young People and Women
10. Intellectual Work
11. A Profession of Faith.

There has rarely been in psychiatry as accomplished a writer as Laing. His comments are challenging, reflecting the extraordinarily wide range of his reading in philosophy, medicine, literature and popular culture. In the course of conversations held over a period of several days, Caretti's questions evoked extended replies by Laing on facts and rumours about his views on the meaning of madness in historical context, the greatness and limits of psychoanalysis and Laing's social phenomenology, especially as it relates to the world of the schizophrenic.

During his time as a hospital psychiatrist, Laing worked with 'back ward' patients who were thought to be incurable. In his private practice he later went on to work with the full range of clientele, some of whom included well-known figures in the arts. Laing's autobiography, *Wisdom, Madness and Folly* (1985) echoes the title of Caretti's book, especially Laing's interest in understanding the meaning of insanity and the need to provide some individuals with an alternative to traditional psychiatric treatment (from electroshock and lobotomy, forced restraint in psychiatric hospitals and medication with so-called 'psychotropic' drugs) and personal isolation. Laing's search for situations in which individuals might be free to live out their madness in small communal settings included the formation of halfway houses such as Kingsley Hall (which he founded in 1965) where patients and therapists lived together with special attention being given to their respective identities. His experiences with LSD (a synthetic drug originally used in the experimental treatment of schizophrenia), explorations of Eastern religious practices and support of a libertarian approach to emotional distress were often controversial, but all of them were grounded in a sober appreciation of the realities of conventional Western medical practice and its ethics.

In the course of these conversations, Laing was prescient in his appreciation of the women's movement as it was developing in his lifetime. So also was his sensitivity to the special place of the adolescent's experience in the unfolding of the life course. To repeat the words of the pre-Christian playwright, Terence, nothing human was foreign to him. His skill as a therapist has been documented on video, including his famous interview in 1985 with a homeless woman in Arizona for a meeting of psychiatrists and psychologists from around the world, but in this montage of reflections presented by Caretti, we have a unique overview of Laing's career as a student, young psychiatrist, radical thinker and a kind of poet among otherwise pedestrian healthcare professionals.

Interest in this work should be wide, especially because of its unavailability in English before now. It also coincides with a renaissance of interest in existential psychotherapy, especially daseinsanalysis, at a time when a remarkable number of people are being prescribed medications for problems in living and the psychiatric approach to mental illness is being challenged vigorously throughout the West. Deeply rooted in phenomenological description and with an uncanny capacity for empathy, in his conversations (and publications) Laing bridges the personal and social, and he finds a central place for the spiritual in psychotherapy during a period of extreme social upheaval and uncertainty. This 'innovation' is perhaps the most remarkable moment of insight in Laing's life and work.

The work we are presenting to the reading public today is the result of much passion and sacrifice, of hard work and study. But it is above all the result of a close and firm synergy between myself and Professors Miles Groth and Vincenzo Caretti, whom I did not know before this incredible publishing adventure and whom I sincerely thank for their support and care towards me. In particular, this translation would never have come about without the coordination, tenacity and perseverance of Professor Groth, who immediately believed in this ambitious project and wanted to carry it out, despite the many evident difficulties and perplexities it held out for us. The participation and constant presence of Professor Caretti further enhanced the translation project, giving it a special meaning. Each time, Professor Groth and I were enchanted by the stories and 'moments of life' that Professor Caretti shared with us in our pleasant and concentrated conversations, stories that primarily concerned his relationship with Laing and the genesis of the interviews published in 1979.

I learned a lot from this project and it has been a real gift to meet people of great experience and sensitivity who have given me a sense of the sacredness of their time. My thanks go to them. At a time when everyone chats and does not know how to listen, they were willing to listen to a young scholar who still has a long way to go and many paths to take. This is perhaps what makes such projects worthwhile: the listening.

Danilo Serra

PREFACE TO THE ENGLISH TRANSLATION (2021)

Today every inch of private space has been invaded and diminished by technology, which in turn is programmed to reproduce and perpetuate upon us the many controls it has imposed on our civilization.

Our modern era has witnessed the extinction of human social thought which during the previous stage of the industrial era raised hopes that human experience could take on new forms. Under these conditions, it is hard to imagine a type of freedom that can exist without its own inherent discomfort or alienation. As a result, the individual as whole has become a virtual abstraction because of this mimesis which conveniently identifies the individual with the technological power controlling him. Even protests and mindfulness no longer contradict this power, having become the ceremonial part of practical behaviourism with its innocuous annulment and readily assimilated part of a healthy diet of the collective conscience. This process makes the manifold nature of human experience seem to be fossilised into almost mechanical reactions set off by the negation of a perspective that is close to nature. Even sorrow and wonder, those emotions philosophers have always considered the source of our need to know and manifestations of existence, have been controlled, tidied up and domesticated by the predictions of science and the truths of faith.

Indeed, science and faith offer the best shelter from the unquenchable need to know, which has gradually become a thing of the past. Thus while unspoken resignation has ruthlessly silenced the voices of difference, it is the exchange value and not the value of the truth that has come to matter. At the same time, our sense of restlessness and alienation has come to be measured in terms of this value, while every other form of inquisitiveness must march to its deathly tune.

Today, it is sad that alienation is often mentioned in psychological terms, but this would not be possible unless the whole person had not first been placed under the all-encompassing jurisdiction of technology. Any request for liberation must stem from an awareness that can no longer emerge because it is always blocked by overwhelming collective convictions which have become the predominant element in each individual's pre-conditioning.

If man has become alienated from himself, it is because he has lost his place with respect to being, and it will not be possible to guide man back to himself as long as this lost relationship is neglected. Likewise, it is useless to search for solutions in the individual or in his changing social or psychic relations. Thus the roots of alienation, far more remote than the negative consequences of the capitalist society, can be found in the way Western thought has touted itself as incontrovertible knowledge of the totality of things and thus believed it could dominate the becoming of nature and of the world.

Modern science, at its most powerful in the form of prediction, is the direct consequence of metaphysics, because man now claims for himself the omnipotence that he once attributed to the gods, and he is convinced that nothing can stop him in his conquest. As he has proceeded from one conquest to another, man has gradually separated the being of things from those things themselves, and each time the values he has attached to the ultimate realisation of his own happiness have far exceeded his capacities. But this happiness, which man has bought with his own conditioning and repression, testifies to the nihilism surrounding Western thought, a nihilism whose goal of universal control and domination requires that everything, which is to say every not-nothing, be a nothing. Man can achieve his passion to become godlike only by thinking of things as no-things, and this is the only way he can find the primal cause and final interpretation of the world that surrounds him.

Western history tells of an uninterrupted sequence of such attempts, all of which are founded exclusively upon the metaphysical inducement that there exists some supreme value capable of allowing all things to be or not to be. This is why even modern science has continued the metaphysical project begun by Plato, whose conception of the Good consisted in this very state of being the cause of everything that is. Thus the philosophers of science are wrong when they say metaphysics is a thing of the past, because science has actually adapted the predictions and interpretations of metaphysics to turn them into an omnipotent awareness of the becoming of the world. Despite even its most materialistic and anti-metaphysical conceptions, Western science is still developing the metaphysical project that has embraced the history of our civilization since the time of the Greeks.

The consequence of this nihilism, this foundation which requires things to be nothing, is an alienation in which all human experience occurs. Any criticism of such alienation that does not take account of this nihilism upon which the history of Western experience since the Greeks has been founded can only repeat the same miseries that have caused our present condition. Even Marxism and psychoanalysis, praiseworthy for having identified this alienation, have proved to be inadequate because they belong to the same form of logic they set out to defeat.

My purpose in these interviews with Laing in 1978 was to examine the philosophical basis of psychoanalysis and psychiatry in a changing world, with their peculiar ways of perpetrating the very bewilderment they propose to cure, just as the illness science tries to combat in the mentally alienated is the same one that inflicts science itself.

In our interviews, which Laing turned over to me at the end of my philosophical studies and at the beginning of my psychoanalytical training when I was twenty-five, and before we got into a criticism of psychoanalytic theory, we made a deal with one quite formidable line of thought, an outlook that has all but derailed the strategy of twentieth-century psychiatry and psychoanalysis, and dramatically upset the professional identity of psychologists and therapists with reference to the work of Ronald D. Laing.

Along these lines, my purpose was to bring out in Laing's narrative the conception of experience as the invisibility of man to man, the declared but as yet unexplored premise of Laing's phenomenology. No one has investigated David Hume's influence on that conception, yet it was the *Treatise of Human Nature* that initially cut Laing loose from safe moorings based on Freudian theory. Sadly, Laing's extraordinary intuitions have not been followed by the founding of a theory of psychic experience that can go beyond the nihilism of previous psychology.

And so these interviews begin where *The Politics of Experience* (Laing, 1967) left off, with Laing addressing the same unanswered questions about human experience. From philosophy to psychoanalysis, to the experience of transcendence, this is the intellectual journey we set out on in the course of a week of conversations at his London house. I still wonder if this path was fully effective then, yet I am convinced that it was very important in order to understand the depth of Ronald D. Laing's thought.

The interviews have been read by many people, but I have to thank Professor Miles Groth for encouraging me to publish them in the SEA series of dialogues, and to Dr. Danilo Serra for his fine translation.

My particular thanks go to Ronald D. Laing who followed my evolution as psychoanalyst and researcher to find the courage to have second thoughts.

Vincenzo Caretti
Professor of Clinical and Dynamic Psychology
Chair of the Master's Degree Program in Psychology, Department of Human Sciences, LUMSA University
Rome, Italy

DIALOGUE 1
From Bible to Zen

Vincenzo Caretti: *If one wanted to describe the development of your research with an image, one could speak of a kind of journey that starts from the demand for a science and arrives at the discovery of a faith. Could you describe this journey starting from your cultural origins?*

R.D. Laing: I do not really agree with the route you have outlined. I would not speak of a linear movement from science to faith. For me it is not a matter of polar opposites. It is not that my thought has undergone an evolution that has distanced it from or taken it away from science: science and, if not faith, a desire for faith were both there from the beginning.

But let us try to establish things in time, as you propose. What was my original cultural horizon? I would say that when I arrived at university, the book I knew best, that I had read most, was the Bible, without any special devotion, but just because it was the most important of all books. Then there was music, probably more important than any single intellectual discipline. At the age of eleven or twelve I was set to go from Glasgow (where I lived) to London on a scholarship to study music. But there was the war and the air raids, and so I stayed in grammar school. There, when I reached the third level, I left science and continued with Latin, Greek and English literature.

Then, at sixteen or seventeen, I began a new cycle of reading. The idea was to try to trace the intellectual history of Europe. The Greek I had learned at school was enough for me to read in the original text: the pre-Socratics, Plato and something of Aristotle. In this way, I was able to familiarise myself, in broad terms, with classical and neo-Platonic philosophy. But the first experience of absolute, total, passionate intellectual involvement was when I encountered Kierkegaard and Nietzsche (in that order and at about the same time). You are never the same after reading Nietzsche. There is – and this is fundamental – his destruction of all idols. There is in him a new ability to see the dual functioning of value systems. There is his scanning of our entire Western ideology and cosmology, and his transmutation of it. When you come to see all this with his almost mathematical lucidity – everything turns upside down, the positive becoming negative, and the negative positive – you find yourself drawn towards a vertiginous vortex, plunged into an absolute void, into a kind of nihilism, both in the moral, ethical and existential sense. You are left with the feeling, implicit or explicit, that there is not an inch of solid ground on which any discourse can stand, and the result is the feeling of an endless abyss.

Caretti: *Were these readings of yours common to the majority of young people of your age, or were there other, more widely read authors?*

Laing: To my knowledge, I was the only one doing such readings. The first time I met another person who was interested in these things was at university, when I was nineteen. She was a French girl and she had read Sartre, Kafka and Camus. She was also very attractive and I fell madly in love with her. I had, it is true, a number of male friends, very close friends, and intelligent people. But they were all Christians. Intellectually, their Christian faith satisfied them, so they were not looking for ontological or metaphysical first principles and indeed were not at all interested in such a problem.

In any case, it was important that I had read Sophocles and the Greeks. And above all it was important that I had read them before I came to know Freud and his Oedipus complex. And it was equally important that I had read Nietzsche before Freud, because then I could see how many themes Freud had derived from Nietzsche. Think about repression, projection and internalisation. And think also about Freud's profound distrust of the ordinary mind and its ability to achieve truth and honesty. His doubts about the evolutionary and adaptive value of truth also come from Nietzsche. In fact, in *Civilization and Its Discontents*, in my opinion, Freud echoes Nietzsche to a large extent. So Freud did not grab me as he might otherwise have done. Indeed, without Nietzsche Freud would have completely overpowered me.

Then I went on to study medicine at university. I deliberately never studied philosophy or psychology in a formal sense as academic disciplines. So I never found myself comparing my own 'etymological' definitions of philosophy (the love of wisdom), psychology (the *logos* of the *psyche*) and theology (the *logos* of the Divine) with the way these disciplines were taught at university. To give an example, I never thought that learning theory (Hull, Skinner and Pavlov) were psychology. My idea was that psychology was the study of the human mind, so I did not differentiate between psychology and philosophy, which is the human mind in its attempt to understand its own situation, including its study of itself. If you stop for a moment to consider the problem of psychology, you cannot avoid finding yourself up to your neck in philosophy at its deepest levels.

When I joined the army as a psychiatrist in 1951, my intellectual baggage consisted of scattered fragments of Western philosophy, including the Berkeley-Locke-Hume triad. I had read Spinoza, especially the *Ethics*. And when I think of the project of a geometry of human relations, his chapter on the slavery of man still fascinates me. His formalisations of human relations were the first I had come across. I was then also familiar with David Hume, a Scottish compatriot. The most important thing I remember is that it was Hume who drew my attention to the fact that we have a mind but we do not know its limits. That's a very curious thing, the mind, because you do not know where it begins or ends, and in what sense it begins and ends. You cannot find the boundary of the mind, nor, therefore, answer the question: How extensive is a mind? And if you can not find the boundary of an individual mind, then it becomes fair to assume – Hume does not say so, but it is an intuition I owe to him – that a single mind has no boundary of its own (in fact we never come to understand it) and is instead a kind of *continuum* – like the physical world – with nodes or receiving stations or transformers, which we call our brains.

Then there was Kant's *Critique of Pure Reason*. At that time, reading it seemed to me to solve the problem (which I found very tormenting) of the bifurcation of reality into phenomenon and noumenon. It probably made an impression on me intellectually for the rest of my life. And the same is true of Hegel's *Phenomenology of Spirit*, which revealed to me the drama of the intrinsic and unstoppable evolutionary logic of philosophical positions. It was in his writings that I first came across the master-slave relationship, and the sceptical and unhappy consciousness. His philosophy of the organic made me think seriously for the first time about the nature of our organic being.

So I had Nietzsche, who was behind Freud. And, along with Freud and Sartre, Jung. Sartre led me to read Husserl's *Ideas*. This reading confirmed me in the idea that in the sphere of that special investigation that was mine, a severely critical and purified vision was necessary if one wanted to succeed in seeing the world as a unity of the given and the constructed. On the one hand, you have to be able to see what you see; on the other hand, you have to be able to grasp the way you see it. Husserl gave me an idea of phenomenology, and enlightened me about Plato in a vivid and immediate way, as had never happened to me before. All this found expression in the first part of *The Divided Self*.[1]

At this point, I started practising psychiatry. I had done six months of neurology in a neurosurgical unit in the army, so I had the opportunity to see what clinical psychiatry was all about in a place like that. Until then, the thought of going into clinical psychiatry had not even occurred to me. I was thinking more about neurology. And there was a kind of phenomenological suspense in me, in the sense that I could not believe that a psychiatrist was really a psychiatrist. The situation seemed to me to be the one depicted by Genet in *The Balcony*. It was nothing more than charade between patient and psychiatrist. And the psychiatric characterisation, modelled on the medical characterisation, seemed very bizarre to me.

It seemed clear to me that the person whom I was, so to speak, examining, looking into her eyes, ears and even her rear-end, and then diagnosing her as suffering from catatonic schizophrenia, she was simply chillingly terrified. And if she had manifested it by screaming, or trembling with fear, it would have been perfectly reasonable to act in such a way as to make her feel that she was in a safe place, where it was perhaps possible for her to begin to loosen up.

If I somehow managed to solve this problem, I owe it largely to Joe Schorstein, one of the few people who influenced me intellectually. Schorstein was a brain surgeon in my unit, and during the war he had commanded the British Army's No. 1 Field Neurosurgical Unit in Africa and Italy. His father had been a Chassidic rabbi not far from Vienna, and also a professional philosopher. So Joe had received a very strict upbringing. He told me, for example, that in atonement for a childhood failing (he was eleven), he was required to read and study the *Critique of Pure Reason*, and then give an account of it to his father. He had a profound knowledge of Plato, Kant, Heidegger and European existentialist philosophy. I had long conversations with him.

Joe Schorstein introduced me to Kurt Goldstein. And another push in this direction came from Merleau-Ponty, whose book *La structure du comportement* was a real godsend for me. The clash between clinical neurology, with all its roughness and intellectual naivety, and the horizon of phenomenological neurology (or neurophysiology) was extremely painful. So the encounter with Goldstein and Merleau-Ponty was for me a great reconciliation and a great relief.

Finally, I came across Sullivan, where he says that between neurology and psychiatry the *mésalliance* is complete: "The name of the discipline is psychiatry, and its field is the study of interpersonal relationships, especially their disorders." I had never heard anyone say such a thing, and I shall always remain attached to Sullivan. It is amazing how useful a formula can be. Until you put it into words, you can never really know a thing. So I understood that the main thing is what happens between people. And psychiatric practice is, more or less, the complete negation of that.

Through Sullivan, the whole world of the American school of interpersonal relations opened up to me naturally. I met Frieda Fromm-Reichmann and others, and became familiar with Adolf Meyer's 'reaction types' and the various nuances of their admixtures. Moreover, when I was later able to devote myself to it at the Tavistock Institute, the whole field of human relations became the subject of a real career.

I have not yet mentioned Tillich, who was extremely important. And Marcel and Binswanger also made a great impression on me. Karl Jaspers had agreed to take me on just before the army drafted me, and I had a vague knowledge of his work in psychiatry. By this time, however, I would say that I possessed the bulk of the intellectual baggage that would accompany me over the next ten years, and which was the basis of *The Divided Self*.

Caretti: *You have already mentioned your encounter with existentialism. But since existential thought and philosophies are the starting point of your 'discourse' on psychiatry, I think it is important to specify how and when you first approached this vision of man.*

Laing: It happened at the end of the war, with the discovery of Camus. At that time I became aware of that French literature of which I had not had the slightest inkling at school. In fact, I was very far from it. At the age of sixteen or seventeen, I was still living in Athens, in classical Greece, and my mind was not attuned to the present. I would say that I did not know a single twentieth-century author, whether philosopher, psychologist, thinker or writer. Of contemporary English literature I knew no more than Eliot's *Waste Land*. I had not even heard of Joyce, and I did not know Thomas Hardy who, I now realise, is much more of a contemporary of ours than Joyce.

In any case, I came into contact with existentialism through Camus' *La Peste*. Then the presence of Kafka and Sartre impressed itself on me, as well as the chilling atmosphere in which their reality is immersed.

Caretti: *How has Sartre's vision of an existential psychology influenced your research?*

Laing: *Being and Nothingness* did not come out until 1951, when I was leaving the army's neurosurgical unit. At that time I was thinking of becoming a neuropsychiatrist and combining this activity with psychoanalysis. I had already read something by Heidegger, which was of decisive importance. And when I met Sartre, the impression was of wearing a tailor-made glove. I can understand that he spent twenty years working on his book. It is his most systematic attempt, and I found it extremely useful, especially the first chapters of Part Three on the relationship with the Other, who is on the one hand the non-personal object or thing, and, on the other, the one who experiences me in the same way that I experience him or her. This is an absolutely basic distinction for me, the clarification of which I owe to these pages of Sartre.

But I had not yet read Husserl, and I needed him to make relevant the skeptical *epoché*. His "suspension of judgement" gave me the concept of truth proper to skeptical philosophy. I did not understand how strict the constraints it imposed were, and, indeed, even when I did understand it, it was in a way that I am sure Husserl would not have considered radical enough. I was never quite able to follow him in his transcendental reductions.

Caretti: *Existentialism, however, has generated contrasting insights, from the deep religiosity of Kierkegaard to the philosophical atheism of Sartre. You, for example, wrote that our civilisation not only represses 'instincts' but also all forms of transcendence. After so many years of reflections and experiences, many of them religious, what is your conception of faith now?*

Laing: Sartre was recently credited with the utterance, "All my life I have tried to be an atheist". Well, the spirit that dictated these words I find very congenial.

I realised very early on that for me there could be no faith, if faith is to be understood as belief in a scientifically implausible hypothesis. If faith meant believing in a story, well, however wonderful or sublime it might be, I could not *believe* in it in the way that seems to be required in certain circles. I cannot imagine myself believing in any verbal formula in such a way as to feel faith. I would rather be thrown to the lions or suffer torture. Rather than affirm that I believe in such a formula, I would accept death. I have never understood what assertions such as "We are saved through the blood of Jesus Christ" really mean. What does that mean? Certainly, expressions of this kind have always awakened in me very deep echoes, but at an intellectual level all uncertainty was erased by the reading of Dionysius the Aeropagite. His negative theology, and in particular the first chapters of *De divinis nominibus*, gave me the solution to the problem. Dionysius lists all the attributes of God that he can come up with: he exists, he does not exist; he is good, he is evil; and so on. And all these attributes (with their negations) are attributes that we impose on God. God is the very foundation that makes possible our ability to define these attributes. So if we are talking about that by which every concept becomes possible, we cannot expect it to be a concept, nor can we expect any concept of ours to give us an image, however ephemeral, of that which is not a concept. That is, in this case we are talking about something that cannot be conceptualised but is the foundation of all conceptualising. Indeed, to say 'the foundation of all conceptualising" is already to conceive what is inconceivable, what cannot be spoken of. It is therefore clear that one must be silent and that one cannot therefore say what one's faith is.

Faith is, in a sense, an intimate relationship with God. It is almost God in relationship with God, so to speak. In this sense, faith is the foundation of our own being. But I do not want to venture even a rough definition of faith. It is, we might almost say, where life is the foundation of our being in communion with the foundation of being itself – the substance of things hoped for by the evidence of things not seen.

I have always felt in myself a lack of faith. I would like to feel that I have more faith. I have often felt something that is perhaps not the opposite of faith, but which I have perceived as a lack of faith: a futility, a meaninglessness, a vacuity, a feeling that in the whole charade there is no ultimate value. Everything was just *vanitas vanitatum*, and so on and so forth. This state of mind was a very typical trait of mine, especially between the ages of twenty and twenty-five. But such moods are reflections of the atmosphere in which we live. I have just read Flaubert, and there I found this way of being represented with a maturity that I did not have then. He offers a great image, that of a sphere that is soft or moist, that has completely dried out or hardened, crystallised or formalised.

Caretti: *This conception of faith of yours is reminiscent of Tillich's theistic vision, his "courage to be". What do you remember about him?*

Laing: Tillich's theism is a complicated and difficult matter. I was told that his American students of the last period could not distinguish his positions from atheism. Sometimes he himself declared that he was not a theist. And listening to him, it certainly happened that I could not distinguish his attitude from that of people ready to profess themselves as atheists. But I am convinced that Tillich never lost the sense of mystery, and this explains why he could not make clear statements, say yes or no, and choose between theism and atheism.

I remember a conversation in Glasgow in which he quoted the passage in the Gospels in which Jesus addresses his disciples, inviting them to say who He is. One says "You are Elijah" and others continue "You are this", "You are that". And Tillich's comment was that perhaps Jesus himself did not know who he was. Tillich was therefore ready to draw the most radical consequences from the doctrine of the Incarnation, of God becoming man. Jesus has forgotten, does not know. Many Christians were deeply disturbed by Tillich's speeches. There was that time in Glasgow when an old woman was sitting next to me. When Tillich finished speaking, she turned to me in tears and said: "It is not right that a man like him should come and destroy the faith of an old woman like me."

Caretti: *Turning to your criticism of traditional psychiatry, do you not think it can be related to your discovery of Buddhist philosophy? Cannot a relationship be established between the existentialist concept of 'nothingness' and the Buddhist concept of 'emptiness'* (Sunyata)*?*

Laing: My understanding of psychiatry was already well-established at least a decade before I became seriously interested in Buddhist philosophy.

Perhaps one can say that I had a smattering of Buddhist philosophy, but nothing more than what is normally found in the knowledge base of a young Western intellectual. In certain Buddhist literature that flourished in northern India and Tibet after the fourteenth and fifteenth centuries an extremely refined intellectual life is expressed. Then there were great Buddhist logicians and so on. But what attracted me most of all was that in Buddhism itself there is practically nothing philosophical. All philosophy has cheerfully self-destructed. We can perhaps say that it is a kind of anti-philosophy.

The core of Buddhism can be summed up in Satipatthana[2] and Vipassana.[3] And the particular form I practised was Anapanasati[4]: concentration on inhalation and exhalation, which in certain Buddhist circles is said to have been the meditation traditionally favoured by the Buddha. It all boils down to the fact that you do not think about anything. You simply concentrate on one point, and continue for as long as you can without doing anything else. In the meantime different transformations take place in your consciousness, and you just notice them and continue to meditate.

Whether this changes your philosophical perspective in any way, I cannot say. But I think the practice must inevitably destroy any philosophical perspective by the mere fact that, during the transformation of experience, it destroys many forms of philosophical naivety. One can go phenomenologically speaking from a seamless subjective idealism to an objective realism in a matter of seconds. So you realise that there are several but perhaps not an infinite number of different ways of grasping the situation towards which you are heading, and on each of them all sorts of philosophies have been built. In a sense, philosophy is an attempt to rationalise a particular fixed way in which the philosopher experiences things. When one understands that all these different positions are experienceable, then one can really read Hegel's *Phenomenology of Spirit*. It is no longer necessary to locate it on an historical continuum. It is now, so to speak, internalised. According to Hegel's image, we revolve through these different states, the wheel keeps turning, and we keep moving from one colouration to another colouration, none of which is really stable, none of which is fixed. Zen affirms that in those things or objects, or at points that we often naively deem important, there is no constancy, no constant substantive reality.

Reality is composed of what we believe to be real. In fact, it is a tale spun from news that comes to us from difference. Information is news of such differences. It is the relationship between the notes and not the notes themselves that gives shape to melody or harmony. You can change all the signs of the notes and yet retain the relationships that bind them. It is the modulation, the form, that counts.

But this modutation, which is made up of the elements that first appeared to us as real, is not itself a thing or a substance or whatever. It is the difference between those things whose presence in fact is only constituted through the texture of their differences. And this may be regarded as a fairly exact exposition of the Buddhist position of the Sunyata, as I understand it. I have spoken in terms of space, but of course there are diachronic differences and synchronic relationships involved which continually evolve over time.

I think that what Sartre does, Buddhists could do. There is no incompatibility. Think of Heidegger's representation of this temporal dimension, especially in the discussion about "what we can say we are". I can barely say "Now" and this moment is no longer the 'now' I was saying a moment ago. That 'now' is now the past, so much so that the past is what we were and are not. The future is in turn what we are not yet, and the present only dissolves continuously. We are filled with this nihilisation of ourselves. We cannot say that we are, nor can we equivocally say that we are not. So we are this particular kind of being that is and is not, that continuously nullifies itself. This is an essential characteristic of existence. But of course the Buddhist position has also dissolved substance into form, and form can only be said to be no-thing.

DIALOGUE 2
The Method of Science and the New Psychology

Caretti: *In* The Facts of Life,[5] *you wrote that scientific interference is the most destructive of all, and that only a scientist knows how to interfere in the most unjust way. But is there any way in which science can intervene in the world without tampering with it and above all ruining it?*

Laing: I think I should first clarify that in that statement I use the word 'science' in a very circumscribed sense. I do not believe, for example, that it applies to astronomy. An astronomer cannot really be said to be trying to interfere with the stars, although a certain kind of scientific spirit would be only too happy to do so, if only it could. I am thinking of that kind of mentality which would not be averse to employing planetary ingenuity to give Mercury a whack and bring it a little closer to the sun. It must also be acknowledged that some anthropologists have been very careful not to disturb the cultures they study. It is not really necessary to take a man belonging to a primitive culture and lock him up in a laboratory like a monkey to see how he reacts. The same can be said of some ethologists, and credit must be given to all those scientists like Goldstein and Merleau-Ponty who are committed to such an approach.

The reality is that we are in a relation of interaction with the world. As a person, I am ready to interact with the world, even though I may have to destroy some of it to make room for myself. A Buddhist story tells of a follower of the Buddha who was blamed for trampling on the grass during the rainy season (since the grass was growing at that time). Well, the Buddha accepted the criticism and suggested that every year we spend those three months just sitting and meditating. This attitude of complete non-contact means that one cannot start a love affair (sexual relations are out of the question), nor interact with others at all. Not only that, one cannot even be interested in such interaction and study it. One cannot even look at it in an attempt to describe it. This is not the kind of involvement we would expect to find in Zen monasteries.

In short, I have two objections to this kind of scientific interference. The first is that it does not tell me what I want to know, and it does not tell me such for the simple reason that it cannot. The second is a moral objection. In The *Facts of Life* I gave an example of William James's way of reasoning in the first volume of his *Principles of Psychology*. If we want to study the human brain, I just do not see how we can do it by torturing a live frog and then cutting it to pieces. In one of his famous essays, Warren McCulloch[6] writes that a frog is a very sophisticated mechanism, but then destroys it piece by piece. Existentially, I am not at all impressed by what the frog's eye or brain can tell us. I distrust the whole Western doctrine of how our bodies work. All our knowledge comes from the study of dead flesh, along the lines of the standard muscle nerve preparation. This is a piece of muscle taken from a living creature, immersed in a saline solution, and then subjected to stimuli in order to study neuromuscular reactions, etc. in order to see how the body works. Well, I could not predict how any fragment of my nerve or muscle tissue would behave after my death or outside the context of my living body. Of course, it would have to be shown to me that it is the same thing. How do we know, for example, that the metabolism of something dead is the same as the metabolism of something living? I know that studying the metabolism of life is technically very difficult. Even when you have a biopsy in view, what you look at through the microscope is a thousand miles away from resembling what it was in the living body.

Then I have a decisive methodological objection, which covers both main objections. I am ethically outraged. I am not willing to admit that our sense of right and wrong is entirely devoid of epistemological value. In other words, can what is morally wrong be scientifically right? If one pursues evil knowledge, perhaps a profound error creeps into one's knowledge. It is an old story, exemplified by the figure of Faust. Nor am I willing to admit that love and solicitude, empathy or sympathy – which it seems fair to argue are not an illusion, but are the real perceptions of an important, fundamental aspect of the nature of the Other – are left entirely aside. As Jacques Monod and others say, if one ignores the basic aspect of the nature of the Other, then science is worthless. It has no inherent principles to limit its exploration, curiosity and manipulation. If we read Bacon and the other early theorists of the inductive method, we see that they are ruthless. In his *Instauratio magna*, Bacon writes: "I mean it to be a [natural] history not only of nature free and at large…but much more of nature under constraint and vexed; that is to say, when by art and the hand of man she is forced out of her natural state, and squeezed and moulded."[7] This is their scientific method.

Now, suppose I want to understand the psychology of women. I do not think the best way to proceed is to cut them into small pieces and speak to them and see how the parts twitch. No, that's not the right way. Instead, it is clear that the way is through polite, civilised speech and conversation. You asked me about my faith. Well, some may be convinced (there have been some in the past) that to ascertain the real nature of my faith, I must be tied to the wheel and see what happens. My objection is both methodological and ethical.

Caretti: *In fact, we still do not know how a brain thinks or remembers, why someone is smarter than another and where the traces of individual memory are. What do you think is the relationship between psyche and brain?*

Laing: I think that if we take the body as a whole and in particular the central nervous system, the integrity of the various parts of the body and its functioning are (within certain limits) together with the whole organism the pre-condition of our ability to manifest our psyche or our mind to others and vice versa. Do you not think so?

Caretti: *Sure.*

Laing: So we agree. Then we can say that an organic state *x* is the pre-condition for the manifestation of our mind, which we call *y*. It is now a question of examining this organic pre-condition. Even if one half of my liver were removed, or my legs and arms amputated, or even my sense organs were destroyed, I would remain perfectly capable of manifesting mind. It may be said, then, that we have no definite or certain idea as to what is the organic pre-condition of memory. And the same is true of consciousness. A manifest action of the mind, however, is impossible unless we were able to hold time together for a handful of seconds; otherwise everything we say would dissolve, run away. If we were to maintain even such minimal control of time, a manifestation of mind would become possible. We can therefore say there is no manifestation of *y* if the organic state *x* is not present, that is, a whole situation that binds the two together. Of course, we may add that besides the organic state there are other pre-conditions. For instance, if the composition of the atmosphere is not the appropriate one or if the composition of our ecosystem were to vary, no manifestation of mind could take place, for we would perhaps find ourselves dumbstruck or in a coma, if not dead. But, regardless of this, it is safe to say that if *y* stands for the manifestation or unfolding of mind, then "if *not-x*, then *not-y*". Or also, "if *y*, then *x*". That is, given some manifestation of mind, there must be (as far as we know) some organic mediation from mind to mind.

Actually, if you think of the field of ESP phenomena, we should rather put this last statement in brackets. I think this is undecidable.

What I want to establish is that, even if *x* is the necessary pre-condition of *y*, this does not mean that *x* causes *y*. In simple terms, we cannot introduce water into our stomach without a mouth, but this does not mean that the mouth is the cause of the fact that there is water in a given stomach. In the same way, one needs a television set to be able to receive and watch programmes. But that is not say the television set is the cause of the programmes. However, we can say that it is the *conditio sine qua non* of the programmes. Thus the possibility emerges that the brain is something like a transistor. It is tuned to different wavelengths – not all of them, just a narrow bandwidth of wavelengths. What we perceive is mediated by the brain, and the brain itself, which we see and touch, is one of the transformers we need to perceive it. Thus, if on the one hand the brain belongs to the class of phenomena, it is also true that it is at the same time one of the transformers that are supposed to be its cause. I have never managed to see a solution to this difficulty. I mean, it is a difficulty that blocks further discourse, checkmates it, makes it opaque. You can certainly say that *x* is a *conditio sine qua non* of *y*. But to go beyond this reasoning and say that *y* is caused by *x* is another matter altogether.

Some people will think these are just sophistical niceties. But in the same way as all the complex metaphysical arguments about psychophysical parallelism, or interactionism, or epiphenomenalism, or the monism-dualism question, you can not blame them for trying to account for the concepts they use and perhaps deciding that they should be put in brackets.

Then there is the phenomenon of psychic synchronicity. I do not think there is a physical explanation for synchronicity at the moment, but that does not mean there cannot be. These things happen every day. For example, two people have two identical dreams at a distance but at the same time. The lives of all of us are probably littered with such events. We just tend to overlook them. For my part, I have made an effort over the past few years to detect precisely all such discernible events.

Jung agonised over this problem, without being able to find a connection or a causal principle. His approach, which is very useful, is more a description of a classical phenomenon than an attempt, we must say, not to explain it but to just understand it. Yet we cannot set it aside or exclude it from the scope of our investigations, even if as soon as we admit the existence of such a class of phenomena we feel all intellectually frustrated because we cannot explain them. We could perhaps speak of a psychosphere, of a psychic dimension that is not located in any of the innumerable specific places in the brain. We may even have to devise a field theory for the mind.

Caretti: *So, with Jung and Nietzsche, do you also believe that the overcoming of science will be a necessary stage of human consciousness? In this sense, what do you think will be the future of psychology?*

Laing: I agree with Jung in his particular use of the term 'phenomenology'. Psychology as a discipline must be given its own specific space and the right to study the phenomena of the mind. It is here that the domestication of the mind, so to speak, intervenes, i.e. the politics of control and limitation of the mind, and the politics of experience. Now, the phenomena of the mind bring us to consider all sorts of situations where the mind proves scientifically embarrassing. From the point of view of physical science in its present state, it is very difficult to establish a link between these two areas of investigation and to account for them.

For example, over the past five years or so the number of people seeking radical therapies of various kinds has steadily increased. One of these therapies is the so-called 'primal therapy' in which the subject relives the experience of his or her birth. Now this is completely inconceivable to the majority of orthodox ontogenetic physiologists and their colleagues. These people cannot imagine how this is possible. But the scandal is actually much more serious, since birth is far from being the last stage in this journey backwards. The process was described two thousand years ago in the manuals and meditations of classical Buddhism. There are those who have traced the course of time as far back as the womb and, before that, as far back as the past bardo plane of existence between their present incarnation and their last death.[8] Many are able to recall their past lives, sometimes with remarkable intensity and richness of detail. These are phenomena experienced as psychologically real (and in some cases as physically real); think for instance of materialisation and the like.

Psychology must have the right to look at all these things, suspending judgement as every epistemologically experienced scientist does as to the ontological reality of the phenomena. Psychology must be free to look at everything that men feel, believe and imagine, not excluding visions, hallucinations and the like, without anyone reproaching him by saying: "This is not valid, this is false; this cannot be and therefore does not happen or should not happen; or that to deal with all this is a waste of time." As I wrote in *The Facts of Life*, such a use of Occam's razor is completely wrong. It does not mean economising hypotheses to cope with the data, but shrinking the data to fit the hypotheses. To dismiss a phenomenon just because one cannot account for it is just not done. In an extreme case, a philosopher like Quine does not hesitate to say that he repudiates the entire field of mental activity. According to Quine, it does not exist, and in his scheme of things neither dreams nor thoughts have any place, so far as I know. There are only inputs and verbal behaviour. How the most radical, extreme of physical behaviourists can justify his position is beyond me.

The starting point, the primary sphere of psychology must be empirical phenomenology. And so, it seems to me that a perfectly valid, highly respectable, and indeed inevitable and important line of enquiry consists in asking what is the nature of the correlation or interaction between this sphere and the sphere of research of the physicist and chemist. But for the moment all we can say is that there is no answer on which the best minds in psychology and science agree. Behind every single theory are people who have spent the best years of their lives in an effort to define it, and yet each theory is different.

One of the main questions I ask myself is whether this kind of problem is decidable or not. If it is, then we should be able to say what can help us reach a decision (i.e. consensus). Take the world of Wilder Penfield's experiments – in which direct stimulation of the temporal lobe produced vivid visions and the creation of entire scenes that had nothing to do with the subject's physical environment – or the recent *The Self and Its Brain*,[9] by Popper and Eccles. Both examples lend themselves to the definition of a multiplicity of undecidable propositions when it comes to what should in fact be considered to be the interrelationship between the domain of the mind and stimulation of the brain.

In any case, the starting point of psychology is phenomenological, i.e. it is the study of experience as it is. This means that psychology is not particularly prone to introspection. It looks at what we see in the world, and also to a certain extent at how we see it, where 'seeing' is to be understood only as a metaphor for the whole synthesis of how we grasp or experience the world in its immediate, dense totality. We thus observe the way we do it, which means that, at this stage at least, psychophysiology has nothing to do with it. Of course, the whole arc of our earthly experience is open to psychological study. Our feelings about ourselves, about the world and society, the way we relate to each other and interact, the data of sociology or anthropology, socioeconomic, institutional, organisational structures – the psychological approach can shed light on all these areas. The way in which we experience these various aspects of our lives as we live them is an inexhaustible subject.

We must then remember that, presumably, we are not talking about some psychological *arcanum*. Otherwise we would fall into pan-physicalism and pan-psychism. In any case, neither affects the other as some have thought. I think it was Thomas Huxley who said: "Consciousness...would appear to be related to the mechanism of the body simply as a collateral product of its working, and to be as completely without any power of modifying that working as the steam whistle which accompanies the work of a locomotive engine is without influence upon its machinery."[10] The whistle corresponds to the psychological dimension. It is produced by the physicality of the engine but does not influence it in any way. It is a one-way process, quite unusual (if not unique) in the world as we understand it. We are faced with products that do not interact with what produces them, that provide no feedback. For example, my brain or my body may produce my feelings, but my feelings as I experience them may have no effect on my body. They are but an epiphenomenon of my organic bodily events.

We are therefore in a situation where psychology and different perspectives are intertwined. Well, as undecidable as these issues appear at the moment, I think that the community of psychologists should not withdraw into psychological arcanum and stop negotiations with what is happening in other fields.

Caretti: *It has to be said here that natural science knows nothing about the relationship between behaviour and experience. You yourself have pointed out several times that the nature of this relation remains 'mysterious' (in the sense of Gabriel Marcel), or, to put it another way, that it does not constitute an objective problem. But what does 'true experience' mean to you?*

Laing: Translating the relationship of what is objective and what is not into an objective problem is impossible. It would be necessary to objectify what is not objective and then compare two objectivities. But in fact the terms of comparison are one subjectivity and one objectivity. So I cannot see how it is possible to compare subjectivity and objectivity by the methods of pure subjectivity or pure objectivity. Perhaps such an angle exists, but I confess it eludes me. And, as far as I know, no one has managed to solve the problem in a truly satisfactory way.

To say that it is mysterious does not seem to me to be of any use. It resolves itself into saying that it cannot be adequately expressed in a formula. There are probably things to which one must resign oneself. But I am not sure that in this case it is an absolute impossibility, but not rather a conditional and contingent impossibility linked to the unavoidable historical limits of our meta-categories. When we say an experience is true or false, we implicitly raise a logical problem and risk a possible confusion between the different uses of the words 'true' and 'false'. Let us suppose that someone sitting in this room feels suffocated or crushed. Physically, he is not suffocating and nobody is crushing him. Yet the feeling may be so strong that he really feels physically as if he is being crushed. This someone might even go further and declare that he is really being crushed and not just in the way he feels or in a metaphorical sense. We all treat our feelings and sensations metaphorically. We are all forced to give linguistic expression to our feelings by resorting to physical metaphors.

But it also happens that the metaphor ceases to be a metaphor. I mean, if I suffer an asthma attack, I really feel suffocated and maybe I really suffocate. The suffocation is therefore real and I might even die. So sometimes we seem to be able to manifest corporeally, to create in our bodies and in our relationship with others a concrete physical realisation of psychological realities. If one feels that another person is annihilating him and what he feels is actually happening on a physical level, we are faced with a very singular state of affairs, similar to that which is created when, in some cases, we seem able to render true our dreams or nightmares.

I speak of such thinking about how difficult it is to determine when a person is, shall we say, 'deluded' and when not. But, granted that difficulty, I think there are an infinite number of possibilities for building on what we experience as constructions that are both false and real. The point is that the construction we superimpose on our experience is itself part of the fabric of what we experience: on the one hand, the false construction in a certain sense falsifies the experience (which is indeed falsely constructed) and, on the other hand, at the same time, it constitutes a particular validation of it.

Caretti: *Some of your critics have said that despite your originality of thought, the object of your scientific research remains confused. Juliet Mitchell[1] has even said that your intentions are more ideological than scientific. What do you think about this?*

Laing: It depends. I think you should give me some more examples of the kind of criticism you have in mind, because I am not sure I would lump them all together with that sort of criticism. I agree with Foucault when he says that we have to accept the historically contingent character of our way of ordering things. In states of meditation (in some cases spontaneous) or under the influence of chemicals (LSD or mescaline or other similar drugs), we can dissolve our usual way of ordering things (down to zero in meditation). But when we return from the zero state, things are again ordered exactly as they were before, and it is likely that we feel more clearly the insubstantiality of arrangement of things if, when it has dissolved and then re-emerged again, we were to be in a state of clear consciousness. We are likely to see this ordering scheme of things as a map of the territory, without confusing the map with the territory. The ineffability and perhaps inaccessibility of the territory remains intact. If the territory is the territory of what is in itself, then it is inaccessible to us. But what, then, is accessible? It is our construction of the territory, incorporated *into* our experience of it, which is itself a first-degree construction. The two dimensions are, in short, constructions of different degrees which combine in an indissoluble (or almost indissoluble) synthesis. Our primary perceptual experience of this room is, in a certain sense, our interpretation of it. It is like taking two balloons equidistant from a neutral background. If we change the lighting, one will appear to us to be moving forward and the other moved backwards. This shows that we interpret all our data and that the very constancy of objects is a construction, as Gestalt psychologists have taught us. Our entire primary perceptual world is inherently an interpretation. But that is not enough. To say that my perceptual world is an interpretation is also an interpretation of this perceptual world. I mean that by calling it an interpretation. I am interpreting it. So the interpretation I make of the first-degree dimension (which is itself an interpretation) is a second-degree interpretation. Is it real? Can I consensually validate it? "Is this a dagger which I see before me/The handle toward my hand? Come, let me clutch thee."[12] I extend my hand to touch it and it is not there since I cannot touch it. I have interpreted my visual impression, a visual phenomenon, and yet it is not there, because I cannot touch it. And since the attempt failed, I say it is a hallucination. If I could touch it, it might still be a hallucination. But if in addition to touching it I could hold it in my hand, and if it had a certain weight and in every other respect made its appearance as a small dagger, then it would be permissible for me to believe that it was a real dagger.

In *The Facts of Life* I gave the example of a man I met in Benares. He was a professor of laser chemistry and I came to know him very well. He told me the following story. He was in Japan researching lasers and one morning an Indian in a *dhoti*[13] came into his laboratory and without introducing himself told him it was time for him to return to India. The professor walked alongside the man to the door. The man put his hand on his shoulder, he felt the weight of his hand, and then, suddenly, as he was looking at him, the man disappeared. This professor of laser chemistry was inclined to believe that this was a genuine case of materialisation, but as he thought that we are all materialisations that are works of spirit this did not surprise him very much.

I suppose that if one is speculatively inclined and is a laser chemistry expert interested in holograms and the like, the possibility of a five-channel coordinated hallucination producing three-dimensional, embodied hallucinatory images should not be inconceivable to him. One could then somehow coordinate the phenomenon with the senses of touch, smell and hearing, and in this case you would have by all appearances the real person. And if you can do that and then to go on to propose the idea that the whole dimension in which our life takes place is a flower in the sky is but one further step – and many have already done so. Everything is actually a hallucination, everything is dust, everything is a beautiful flower in the sky. So this is an answer to ideology. You may well call me a naive ideologue. And I admit that the way we order things – that is, our ideology – is, as far as we know, historically conditioned. I imagine that if I lived in a different world or in Egypt at the time of the Middle Empire, I would probably see things differently or perhaps perceive things that I do not perceive now.

Caretti: *And is this not precisely the trap of ideology? Is there any way to avoid it?*

Laing: It would make a difference if I had grown up in Italy rather than here in England and a huge difference if I were an Italian today, or if, say, I had been raised in an African tribe. Especially in *The Politics of the Family* (but it is a thread that runs through all my books) I have made it clear that what really interests me is to look as far as possible at the way we look at things. So my attempt is to reveal to myself and to others our more subtle presuppositions, as distinct from those of a more obviously coarse, ideological nature. I have, however, resigned myself to the immanence of my own investigation. It cannot proceed from a transcendental position outside the system I am investigating. Instead, the investigation is intrinsically part of that system. Similarly, when I investigate my own investigation, I nevertheless remain within it, and so on. But I think there are various degrees of disenchantment, disillusionment, demystification. Certainly each particular degree of demystification, revealing another nuance in the ordering scheme of things, risks crystallising into another ideology. But I do not think I have fallen into that trap.

Caretti: *Earlier you used an expression common to Marxism, 'historically conditioned'. Yet you are critical of it, especially in* Reason and Violence[14] *when you argue that the Marxist dialectic invents a nature without man...*

Laing: I will venture an analogy. Very rough, like all analogies. Let us take the area of what we might call ideological and psychosocial realities, that is, the realm of the products of the human mind, including the theories and speculations of that very mind, and dreams and visions, as well as the stories we tell each other, and the accounts we tell each other about how things are, the stories we tell each other about other stories, and so on. Well, we can say that to a certain extent this area presents the same problems with respect to socioeconomic realities as the field of individual psychology does with respect to the dimension of the organic and the body. And generally Marxists have adopted a position that we might call sociological epiphenomenalism; that is, the idea that the ideological level, in a broad sense, is a product of socioeconomic, physical and material conditions. As the word itself implies, theirs is an 'historical materialism'. So it is yet another form of reductionism, of one-way causation. If, in fact, you credit the mind with an effective presence in the world within its own field, it becomes difficult to accept the conception of those who dogmatically insist that if matter is the cause of the psyche, the psyche has no influence on matter.

Once you have built a system of feedback or reciprocity of some kind, or some sort or dialectic or a cybernetic model, you no longer have any reason to be an historical materialist. In this case, it seems to me, it is very difficult to claim to be Marxist (extending the qualification of Marxist to all investigations of systemic interrelations and interactions within a society, as Lévi-Strauss does). I believe that Lévi-Strauss once declared himself to be a Marxist, insofar as no one can fail to be a Marxist if Marxism is understood as the scientific study of society, with a particular focus on its socioeconomic aspects. Well, I have never been an ideological Marxist in this sense.

In fact, I do not believe that I am primarily an ideologue. If I am an ideologue, then someone will have to tell me what my ideology consists of, because I do not acknowledge one. As mentioned earlier, however, I acknowledge that behind my way of acknowledging there is a deeply programmed and historically conditioned ordering scheme of things. When I say 'historically conditioned', I am not thinking exclusively of material-historical conditions. For example, the intellectual influence of Plato was a very strong one on me, even though he lived in very different socioeconomic conditions from those in which I found myself when I read him or find myself now. And now I do not see why the kind of family one grows up in – a working-class family, say, or one of rich capitalists, with their consequently different social positions – should necessarily influence one's propensity for idealism or realism. Of course, if I had grown up in China, within the present social organisation of that country, I would not have had the opportunity to engage in such speculations. Given the ongoing process of transformation of socioeconomic forms, perhaps a space will open up for so-called freedom of thought, at least in certain limited respects. Of course, some Maoists will reply that by going so far as to say these things, I am indulging in subjective, putrified, idealistic illusions of the worst kind. But how can I manage to say that I am not an ideologue? Come to think of it, in that sense no one can claim *not* to be an ideologue.

Caretti: *In your latest books, you prefer to express your thoughts and emotions in literary forms. Does this tie in with the lines of your most recent scientific research or have you moved on to literature?*

Laing: The scientific method seeks to achieve reliability or validity through its specific type of discourse, where saying scientific method is the same as proclaiming a certain scientific ideology. If you take a dream, and a Jungian and a Freudian make two different interpretations of it – in fact if you have a dozen different people, say a therapist inspired by Gestalt psychology, a Rankian, a Reichian and so on – all will make a dozen different constructions on the same dream. Well, this difference or lack of reliability of the interpretive work tends to invalidate the whole theory. If a theory is tested, one expects first of all to be able to describe the same thing in the same way, rather than to end up with a multiplicity of descriptions. My field is precisely one of a multiplicity of descriptions. Think of the Japanese film *Rashomon*. There it is the same thing. The centre of my interest is the plurality of perspectives. What I am looking for is the difference between the different ways in which the same situation is experienced. Of course, even though it is never experienced in the same way, in order not to abandon common sense, we will still say that it was the same situation. But we are forced to say that it is always experienced and described differently. So looking at the convergence and divergence of these different perspectives, it appears that there are different ways of conveying our own perspective (which in this case is a meta-perspective). This is what every novelist does; that is, he takes the perspective of a multiplicity of perspectives, and his personal perspective is itself included in that multiplicity. This presents serious problems of literary method. Sartre blamed François Mauriac for assuming the visual perspective of a God. Or think of the novelist who takes the position of all his different characters, describing situations from each of their different perspectives. Well, that can be done only in the imagination by constructing a novel or a book. To give an example: no one will ever be able to confirm what Raskolnikov really felt – whatever it was – as he set out to commit his crime.

There are thus many ways in which we can try to give expression to different perspectives and some of them are not usually considered part of the scientific lexicon (although sometimes they are). If you happen to see Konrad Lorenz, the ethologist, giving a lecture, you will notice that when he talks about geese or chimpanzees, he assumes with extremely effective mimicry the manner of a goose or a chimpanzee. In other words, Lorenz does not restrict himself to the techniques of scientific discourse at all. Even at the Royal Society, where I once happened to meet him, I heard him speak in a way that I would describe as digital communication. His was a performance, mimesis, a dramatic, visual analogue. Mimicry, imitation, identification, stage acting – all these elements are part and parcel of Lorenz's scientific discourse. But scientists have been inclined to devalue the scientific importance of some of the most valuable components of their own way of communicating. Let me give you an example. A few weeks ago I was in Florence listening to physicists talking about the Big Bang Theory trying to convey to the audience their notion of physical reality. Now, everyone was gesticulating very animatedly, even when they were talking about their most abstract equations. They were communicating, so to speak, in terms of their bodily movements. These movements created a dynamic visual topology in the form of a gesture. And the curve of an arm's movement tries to convey a tradition in terms of the geometry of physical movement, of the transformation that was the objective of their argument. It is extraordinary to see a very broad abstract cosmological theory expressed in concrete terms through the metaphorical possibilities of human movement. Like a bee trying to make its universe understand itself, here is this little pile of atoms that forms a human being striving to convey to other human beings – this singular form of life that we are – what for him is the image of the universe. In other words, science, like communication and meta-communication, or linguistics and paralinguistics, is a parascientific discourse. I say this only to establish the idea that science is not the so well-defined and nuance-free realm it may seem to be, even when it comes to pure science. As I have said, there are forms of expression, manners of showing, explaining, manifesting, etc. which do not fit into scientific language but which, in my opinion, are compatible with it. And I have decided, exercising my right of choice, to make use of them. If I had the gift of musical composition I would express myself in music; if I had the gift of painting, by painting or sculpting, and so on. But my scientific field is the different ways in which words – and particularly printed words – can be used to signify what one wishes to communicate. For me, the fact that these ways do not always fit into the language of science does not create any conflict

DIALOGUE 3
With Freud and After Freud...

Caretti: *Your disappointment with the psychoanalytic method is evident from the very first pages of* The Divided Self. *Like any disappointment, it hints at a previous enthusiastic adherence. At what age did you begin your analytical training and how did you arrive at your current views on psychoanalysis?*

Laing: I remember that I first turned to the Institute of Psychoanalysis in London for analytical training. I was twenty-one years old and in the middle of my medical studies. In fact my training took place between 1956 and 1960.

I did not know – and do not know even today – any other corpus of writings and investigations that strives to do what psychoanalysis strives to do. For me, the core of psychoanalysis is the relationship between two people who are together in a room for a fixed period of time, under multiple and varied conditions defined in a very rigorous way. It is a formidably simplified and formally repeatable procedure, and it struck me from the beginning as a stroke of genius. It seemed to be a possible, and very clear and elementary, way of simplifying conditions so that they could be more or less the same everywhere. Different people could thus put themselves in such a situation, and sharing the experience of what results, perhaps arrive at some valid scientific generalisations about how and what we feel. Or explain when and why we do not feel, or think and imagine. In a word, it seemed possible to draw some conclusions about the emotions and physical sensations we experience, and indeed about the way we experience absolutely anything and everything. And what results from the method can be identified and defined. So I made the firm decision to become an expert in the use of this particular method, independently of any other method besides it I might wish to learn.

As for the theory that emerges from the experience of the analytic situation, the first thing to say is that there is no unified corpus of psychoanalytic theory. As is well known, even Freud changed his opinion several times on several important questions and vacillated on others. He judged that the different opinions, the oldest and the most recent, were compatible with each other. But other psychoanalysts disagreed. Not only that. Freud saw irreconcilable contradictions where other psychoanalysts saw the possibility of reconciliation. In short, what happened is that every single aspect of Freud's theory, including the very existence of metapsychology, has been repudiated by individuals who were fully-fledged members of the International Psychoanalytical Society, and to whom one cannot therefore deny the sociological qualification as psychoanalysts. Thus among psychoanalysts we find people as diverse as Jules Masserman, Lawrence Kubie, Medard Boss, Wilfred

Bion, Melanie Klein, Ronald Fairbairn, Heinz Hartmann, Ernst Kris, etc., as well as many others. What is orthodoxy in one school of psychoanalysis is anathema in another. Probably only Americans believe in a conflict-free sphere of the ego and a delibinised ego. And surely only Kleinians (a small group, but spreading all over the world) believe in that particular version of child development which is preached by the Kleinian school. As for Lacan and the Lacanians, they cannot find a stable position anywhere.

Each existing school operates at its own singular sophisticated level of ingeniousness and only within the these limits can its members fully agree. Thus it is practically impossible to assert the existence of a theory that qualifies as the psychoanalytic theory. Personally, this does not bother me much, but it presents serious problems in terms of the epistemology of its method and the interpretative categories of psychoanalysis (assuming that there is a psychoanalytic way of interpreting, or construing, phenomena). Indeed, there are serious unresolved problems. Or at least they seem unresolved to me. Nor among any one of them have I found any satisfactory solution so far.

Caretti: *Would you like to explain the differences between the different schools of psychoanalysis a little more extensively? Is there really no theoretical element that is shared by all of them?*

Laing: I find it difficult to point to a single item in the psychoanalytic vocabulary that is not controversial.

For example, the whole project of metapsychology is contested by theorists like Boss and others. In my opinion, these theorists remain within the boundaries of the psychoanalytic movement, but they consider themselves rather as phenomenologists. In fact, the phenomenological branch of psychoanalysis completely repudiates the metapsychological enterprise – except as a metaphor, which is considered pleonastic and a possible source of confusion – because it makes no contribution to the intelligibility of the phenomena in question.

Regarding metapsychological formulations, we include those analysts who retain in one way or another something of the libido theory. However, it should be pointed out, there are those who accept the first formulation of the libido theory but do not admit the existence of an analogous death drive. They do not accept the idea of a *mortido* interacting with libido. On the other hand, Federn (to whom, if I am not mistaken, we owe the term *mortido* to designate the energy of the death drive) and others with him accept this dualistic theory of drives. Yet another group rejects *in toto* Freud's thoughts on drives in all their versions, judging them as nothing more than old-fashioned nineteenth-century materialistic biology. They have substituted refined ethological notions such as innate triggering mechanisms for drive theory, thus completely dismissing the old comprehensive notion of antithetical drives. There are also those who are convinced that the repudiation of Freudian drive theory is based on a mere verbal misunderstanding. It is possible to translate the Freudian term *Trieb* with concepts such as desire in a way that Lacan reconciles with a reading of the master that most Freudians have never even dreamed of. It escapes me at this moment how exactly Lacan renders *Trieb* – it must also be said that he introduces numerous nuances.

There is also object relations theory with its different versions. And there are the interpersonal psychoanalysts, such as the Sullivan school in America and the William Alanson White Foundation, who think that object relations cannot be used to conceptualise the interaction that takes place between two living persons. From this point of view, Frieda Fromm-Reichmann criticises the entire corpus of Freudian theory, which she says is characterised by what she calls a single body psychology. Fromm-Reichmann strives to replace this type of psychology with a two- or three-body psychology, that is, with a psychology of what happens within a multiplicity of people. And it seems fair to say that Freudian theory does not cover these situations.

Finally, there are many other nuances in contemporary psychoanalysis, many of which are defined by mutual opposition, that is, in a negative way. I do not think there is a single settled notion in the whole corpus of theory, not even the notion of the unconscious, which is very problematic from a phenomenological point of view. (Boss devotes long consideration to it, as does Binswanger.)

The problem is that, given such a simple method, which can be reproduced all over the world, and indeed has been reproduced hundreds and thousands of times, one would expect a certain consensus. Here is a room in which there are two people seriously engaged in trying to understand the mind of one of them through his transference to the other. Lacan would say that he is trying to read this person, not unlike reading a book where the text is the patient's unconscious, structured, as it were, like a language that expresses itself without the knowledge of the patient himself and in his conscious expressions. That is fine. This is what we all do. Hundreds, indeed thousands, of people meet two-by-two in as many rooms in Rome as in Los Angeles, in Paris as in Stockholm. But if at the end of the year analysts got together and compared their notes, the most diverse contrasts would result and the dividing lines between all the different schools we have just mentioned would emerge. It would be a Tower of Babel. Suppose, on the other hand, that a group of laboratory researchers agreed to carry out the same experimental work for a year, following the same procedure, and then meet for a conference. If at this point the same diversity of perspectives on an object of research we have seen characterises psychoanalysts were to emerge, I am certain that our researchers would be disconcerted, indeed seriously alarmed or lost. This is not to say that there are not groups of analysts who use the same interpretative categories to a great large extent, but only that there will always be other groups made up of people who are comparable in terms of length of training and working methods who build very different interpretative constructions using the same data.

One would like to be able to find a precisely defined criterion of decidability. Once an agreement has been reached about this criterion, it should be verified whether we have all decided in the same way or not. And, if a divergence is found, it should be possible to rethink the very object of our reflection to see whether by chance it is not different from what we had supposed. It seems to me that what is needed is to take a step back from the dispute, to go beyond saying: "Well, clearly you see things that way." Instead, we must say: "The thing has been seen in this way and therefore you may see it in that way, that that way is a just one way of seeing the thing." Let us call it A. But there is surely another way of seeing it which is the exact opposite of A. Let us call it A_1. In effect, we can say that as soon as we see something in a certain way, this something can immediately be seen in the opposite way. And if other parameters appear on the horizon, other pairs of representations appear: B and B_1, C and C_1, and so on. There is thus a potentially infinite series of ways in which one person (among several) can report what has taken place in the transference.

We could turn the current scientific dogma on its head and say that two descriptions are better than one, and three are better than two; in short, the more descriptions we have of the same thing, the more interesting the problem becomes. The problem is in the first place a problem of description. It is a problem of construction and description of the construction we have made. So what we are looking for is probably to be found in the area of understanding the interaction between these different constructions and descriptions. And precisely this could be a description of the object of psychoanalysis, namely, the description of the co-existence of a multiplicity of perspectives in the absence of a transcendental criterion that makes it possible to decide between them. With the result that one yields to the other, one tries to overwhelm the other. One suppresses, another represses, a third engages in all sorts of activities to overcome the conflicts, the paradoxes, the dissonances of various kinds between the different ways in which we see things.

Caretti: *The multiplicity of perspectives to which you referred earlier refers to the relationship between one's 'inner unity' and the 'unconscious', which is examined in your works. Would you like to clarify the dynamics of this relationship?*

Laing: A totality/unity can be defined as a whole that is presupposed by each of its parts. Well, I am convinced that I am unconscious of most of what my inner unity consists in. It is unconscious or, as Freud says, *unbewusst* (unknown). I do not know where my words come from. I have no idea of the mental operations whose unfolding enables me to say what I am saying at this moment, these very words that I am uttering now. Nor do I know what I will say in a moment. Yet there is a constraint (of which I am unaware) which shapes what I utter, compelling it to be the complete sentence that will have been formulated. But how it will have been formulated I will find out only after it has been spoken. I am unaware I am listening to my own words. I do not know where they come from, nor does anyone else. It often happens to me in every area of life that I only find out why I have done a certain thing long after I have done it. For example, I may go out one day to buy a couple of notebooks. But only when I start writing does it make perfect sense: the number of pages more or less corresponds to certain forms of thought I wanted to put down on paper. In effect, so to speak, I did not know how to purchase a frame until I had finished the painting. In other words, I had to find a frame to fit the painting. At any given moment I am unaware of the inner unity of my memories. I do not recall some single thing, some single memory. I am focused entirely on what I am saying, I am not recalling my life as it is present in my memory. So all those memories are in a sense virtual or available. They are just there, ready to be recalled. But I do not know where and on what they are based, or what sort of existence they have, or what transformations they undergo before they present themselves to me on demand, before they appear, like a *Darstellung*, before my mind's eye. Suppose I want to think of something that happened when I was two-and-a-half-years-old. It is an image that presents itself to me, like a photograph of myself. I am looking at myself. I am remembering something. But it is something that has never actually happened to me, because I have never really seen myself as I am remembering it. In short, everything we focus on is implicated in a background of which we are unaware.

Caretti: *Coming back to the tower of Babel constituted by the different schools of psychoanalysis, do you think it is possible to find a way out of this* contrast *of theories? And how?*

Laing: First of all, I feel I must define, as far as I can, the theoretical problem posed by this contrast of theories. If one lives in a tower of Babel, one possible way of adapting to the situation consists of investigating it. And if I try to investigate it, it seems to me that several problems emerge on the horizon that are not at all trivial and perfectly susceptible to scientific analysis. I think that Gregory Bateson's work on what he calls our "epistemological errors" – and in particular the breadth of the Double Bind Theory – offers a theoretical model that allows us to approach the analysis of communication in formal terms. For example, you can make a film or a videotape and then point out a particular thing (or things) that you can see when you watch the film. At this point, anyone can watch the film, and say whether what is said to be pictured actually does or does not appear in it. It is then possible to give a formal description of what is said to appear in the film. With this we have the tools for a scientific study of communication, as long as we limit ourselves to questions that admit of an answer. I mean if you ask a silly question, you will get a silly answer.

An example of this is a hypothetical experiment I mention in *The Politics of the Family*.[15] Take a group of people institutionalised and categorised as schizophrenics, it makes no difference how. What matters is that you have a number of people categorised as to the extent, or degree, to which they appear to be schizophrenic (forget about whether they actually are or not). Then place the persons so categorised in pairs, each pair with a fellow wearing a white coat, with all the symbols of medical authority. Then have the subjects be examined by this guy in the way a doctor examines a schizophrenic. Meanwhile their reactions are categorised. Then take the same group of patients and categorise their reactions in a situation where they are interacting with another person who is neither dressed nor behaving like a doctor, but appears to be an ordinary person. Finally, compare the categorisations that measure schizophrenic behaviour in the two situations. Well, I am convinced – it is a conviction that comes from twenty years of experience, and which I share with many others – that the experiment would give the following result. When the alleged schizophrenic is treated as a schizophrenic, the schizophrenia index is ten times higher than when he is treated as an ordinary person. This is a very feasible experiment whose results (only apparently conjectural, since, I repeat, my own and other people's extensive experiences in this direction) say a lot about the sensitivity of the symptomatology to the interpersonal environment.

It is also extremely interesting that, to my knowledge, the experiment has never been carried out, despite it being so simple to do. A similar experiment in the field of physics or chemistry would be performed immediately and repeated all over the world. If, on the other hand, no one can be found in the field of psychiatry who is willing to test such a hypothesis, it is because its implications are too disturbing for those who are in a position to carry out the experiment, and who would find themselves displaced and even expelled from their profession by its results. They would have to admit that they were driving their patients mad. It is therefore perfectly understandable that they are not willing to produce evidence against themselves. But from a methodological and scientific point of view, the experiment is solid and feasible. It is confirmable and non-confirmable. And this is by no means the only issue. If I do not do these things myself at the moment, it is not because I think they are trivial or unfeasible, but simply because my interests now lie in other directions.

So let us consider not a single mind, but two minds in relation to each other. Agreed? Here's another interesting experiment. Take a couple – say husband and wife, boyfriend and girlfriend, mother and child, etc. – and subject each of them separately to an intelligence test. Let us say it is a husband and wife, and the husband gets 135 and the wife 140. So we put them together and say, "We would like you to put your minds together, and give us, for the questions of this other intelligence test, joint answers." Now, the important point is that by working together the two of them can get very diverse results: 110 or maybe 160. You can film them, you can record their conversations and you can see how these two people struggle to find ways of seeing the same thing, how one overpowers the other's construction or submits to it, or how they agree to recognise a difference of opinion. By putting their heads together, some destroy themselves intellectually. Others enhance their mental powers. It is an experiment that would be very interesting to do in the Pentagon, in the palaces of power, in committees of all kinds, wherever there is a group of people who hope that by putting their heads together they will reach a better outcome than each of them would get in isolation. This could be done at La Roche, or anywhere else, to see whether the individuals under consideration enhance each other's imaginative faculties or destroy them, or whether their competitive efficiency is enhanced or diminished when they join heads. Or one can also look at how they behave and at all the nuances of the interplay that takes place between them; for example, how a wrong answer can come to be accepted as right by both. In the field of interpersonal interaction and perception, there is a great deal that can be done, all of which is actually feasible and all of which has scientific respectability.

Instead of laboratory experiments, it would be possible to devise situations that set up real games. For example, one could examine the interpersonal interaction of truth and lies and deception and pretending and physiological stress in relation to being deceived – or deceiving – in a situation experienced as a game. Some think that a humanistic psychology precludes such initiatives as creating structured situations, formulating hypotheses and testing them on empirical data, and so on. I, on the other hand, am convinced that it is a perfectly respectable, interesting and non-trivial field of investigation. I know a lot of people who complain about the theoretical confusion we find ourselves in. But if they really want to get serious, this field offers endless topics for doctoral dissertations.

Caretti: *In* The Politics of Experience *you wrote that "psychotherapy must remain an obstinate attempt of two people to recover the wholeness of being human through the relationship between them."*[6] *From this perspective, empathy and understanding would be the basis of any therapeutic relationship. Could you clarify what it means for you to consider the patient not as the object of a research but as a 'Being-in-the-world'?*

Laing: I simply mean that, seen in this way, the Other is exactly one like me. He is another I, not different from me. He is to himself in the same way that I am to myself. He is, in short, the relationship between you and me. This means that I can put myself in your place and you in mine. If each of us treats the other with the same consideration with which we would like to be treated, we would probably not make any great mistakes.

It is a specific problem in the training of the doctor that Foucault described so well in *The Birth of the Clinic* and *Discipline and Punish*. We are taught to observe the patient and our model is a corpse. So first we have the dissection of a body and the examination of a surface. Then, on tearing away this surface, other surfaces appear, and then organs and tissues and all sorts of processes, as we can observe them in laboratory specimens. And here is our patient, who is almost reduced to a thing we put under observation and examine. The surface we observe crosses, as it were, the direction of our gaze at right angles. Given surface AB, we look at it at an angle of ninety degrees. What passes between us and the subject is limited precisely to this ninety-degree angle. If we have been trained for a long time to proceed in this way, changing becomes difficult. Of course, if I have appendicitis or a toothache or whatever is wrong with my organism, I have no particular interest in being treated as a person through a personal relationship. If they just look at my body and that is it, I am fine with that. What I want is just certain manipulations to save my life or to improve it in this or that specific respect. In short, there is something to be said in favour of that way of seeing and examining, of the professionalisation and institutionalisation of that gaze. But when we move on to the field of psychiatry or psychoanalysis, the disturbance must be sought not in an object to be looked at or examined but in the relationship between the person being looked at and the person looking. Thus, if we have only cultivated the first situation, we may find ourselves caught in a trap and may find it very difficult to return to the horizonal and relational situation. Moreover, if we only look at an objective surface and the density within it, it is not possible to sympathise or empathise, or to feel – or be – together with that person. This possibility only arises within and through a relationship with the Other. I am not quite sure that 'empathy' is the right term, nor am I sure that I accept the existence of empathy. If I have a toothache and I talk about it, you can treat me with solicitude and consideration, i.e., with sympathy. If you are a dentist or a sometime neighbour, you may treat me harshly with ruthless disregard. But in neither case do I expect you to feel my pain. I do not expect you to take on my toothache. If I feel miserable and you feel happy, you may remain happy and yet pity my misery, but I will not expect you to take upon your shoulders the burden of my suffering. Or, if it is you who feel miserable, that is no reason for me to be miserable, too, or even for you to have feelings of looking after/caring for, of sympathy, of brotherly comradeship for the unhappy condition in which you find yourself. As long as I see misfortunes around me, my happiness is likely to be clouded by them. Perhaps one cannot be entirely happy. I am not sure. It is a situation that Nietzsche outlines in the *Genealogy of Morality*. He sees in sympathetic communion a principal indication of the degeneration of modern morality.

Caretti: *In psychoanalysis, however, what matters is the value of interpretation. If, for you, empathy or feeling are the necessary aspects of any therapeutic relationship – and here Mitchell warns that the Laingian therapist risks becoming a good consoling mother – then what is the role of the analyst?*

Laing: It seems to me that there are two things to be said. One is that if I do not have, in one way or another, a feeling for the feeling of the other person, I will hardly be able to construct a correct or even a relevant interpretation of the feelings I attribute to him. Now, I am able to talk to terrified people even though I do not know why these people are terrified. But I think this is greatly facilitated by the fact that I am very familiar with my own experiences of anguish, which I cannot relate to any specific occasion. If I lacked this realm of personal experience (although everyone's has its own individual tone), I do not think I would be able to talk to someone in a state of anguish in a way that would make sense to them. And yet people have described to me a number of states that I have never experienced and, in some cases, can barely imagine. Certainly, many of these states I do not want to imagine, nor do I attempt to do so (although it would probably be better for the other person if I could).

There is therefore a first level of attribution, followed by a second level, which is the construction that we superimpose on the attributed state or feeling. I will give you an example of this problem covering a very wide range of situations. In a clinical seminar, a psychoanalyst told of one of his patients who had had the following dream:

> *There were two rock walls facing each other at a certain distance; in the middle a bottomless abyss. Halfway up one of the walls a little door opened and out of it came a*

cuckoo, which made its cry: "Cuckoo! Cuckoo! Cuckoo!" and then, like a cuckoo clock, went back into the rock. Then the same thing was repeated on the other wall.

The analyst interpreted the dream as an expression of the patient's intrapsychic state. He said that the patient was split in two, and each fragment or wall was a cuckoo bird, which is an English way of saying crazy. He was thus trying to make contact with himself across an insuperable abyss. As soon as I heard this dream, I had what one might call an empathic feeling. By that I do not mean a feeling of empathy, but a feeling of how the other person might feel if I had had a dream like this. Like that feeling, my immediate intuitive interpretation of the dream was that it stated that the analyst and the patient were separated by an abyss. And that, faced with this state of non-relationship, both were simply sending meaningless sounds to each other. The psychoanalyst completely rejected this interpretation of mine, arguing that a dream portrays an intrapsychic situation. (According to dogma, a dream first of all portrays a situation between the person who has it and himself, no matter whatever other psychological dimensions it may have.)

How can one decide between two such interpretations? Of course, in analysis the interpretation would be submitted to the patient, whose reaction would confirm or disconfirm in the analyst's eyes his interpretation. But in reality this is not so, because if the patient agrees with the analyst, his may be a pseudo-assent, i.e. given not because the interpretation seems true to him but because he wants to believe it to be true. Or he may accept it because he has been told so. If, on the other hand, the patient disagrees, his disagreement may be an expression of resistance, in which case it still sounds like confirmation to the analyst. In short, if you agree with me, I am right, and if you deny what I say, your denial is worth a reversed affirmation, so I cannot be wrong. I always express any attribution as to how the other person feels by saying that he gives me the impression or the sensation of feeling this way or that way. But I make no claim that my feeling of what the other person feels is necessarily true or even close to being true. In fact, the way I feel that the other person is feeling may be the way he wants me to feel and may not coincide at all with the way he actually feels. It could very well be a feeling that the other person has induced in me about what he or she feels without it even remotely resembling what I actually feel. And when it comes to the possibility that in this field our sensations correspond to the truth, I am very sceptical. All theatre and ninety percent of literature present us with situations in which characters completely misunderstand the reality of their feelings in even the most intimate moments (and often do not grasp the truth, nor could they).

Caretti: *Erich Fromm argues that knowledge of Zen can be very fruitful for psychoanalytic theory and technique. You yourself have come to the conclusion that Zen is a possible therapeutic model.[17] Can you tell us how it is possible to use Zen in therapy?*

Laing: It is impossible to use Zen. I mean, Zen is not something to be used. If and to the extent that the therapist achieves perfect attention and presence, whatever he says or does will be Zen. But Zen cannot be activated or deactivated. It is not like turning a light bulb on or off. You cannot, for example, use Zen to walk, but if you walk, let us say, in a Zen way, then that is Zen. And if you stand, sit or lie down, if you gesture, move or speak (whatever comes out of your mouth), the same applies. I would certainly say that the ideal Zen master would be the perfect therapist and, conversely, the perfect therapist would be the perfect Zen master. No matter what the difference in forms. Everything can be Zen – a motorbike, a round of golf or tennis, boxing or archery, swimming or breathing, or anything else – even if it is only that extreme simplification of sitting still, looking at the wall straight ahead. What characterises this condition as Zen is not sitting looking at the wall. I mean one could just as well take a walk, or anything else. Just by sitting and looking at the wall, you do not come the least bit closer to Zen (nor do you move away from it). Doing a certain thing by concentrating exclusively on it seems to me to be a good exercise, and this for hours every day for several years. When he plays the piano, Horowitz is a Zen master. No Zen master would ever want to confine Zen to a particular historically conditioned social form. But whatever form the Zen mind runs encounters it will inevitably always be a form shaped by the historical moment.

Caretti: *Is a more precise definition of Zen not possible? Perhaps from your own experience of Zen meditation?*

Laing: I have had direct experience of Zen in the form of Zazen meditation. There is a Zendo[18] down the street, and there are usually two Japanese Zen masters present. I send down a bunch of people who achieve great calm and balance in a situation where they just sit and do nothing. They just watch or focus on a particular centre of gravity in the body, or even just look straight ahead. All these procedures, including Koan[19] procedures and the like, are special forms developed in China and Japan, and in themselves cannot tell us what Zen is. It is not even possible to talk about the experience of Zen. If you talk about it, a kind of form emerges, a fragment of the global experience, which cannot immediately coincide with Zen precisely because you have defined it. If you want to talk about Zen in a safe and sure way, you can only say and repeat that you cannot talk about it. You can allude to it but never enunciate it directly. Any positive definition of Zen is immediately and completely non-Zen, including this one I have just articulated.

Caretti: *The main assumptions of Zen are immediacy and intuition. It is said that Zen masters used to throw their disciples into the mud, because they said that mud is more important than words. Have you ever metaphorically thrown your patients into the mud?*

Laing: Metaphorically, I have torn my patients to pieces, beaten them, chastised them in every way. I have shamed them, I have thrown them into shit and rubbed their noses in it, I have stepped on them and so on. The point of all this is not about the use of a Zen method, and there is no theory behind it (although it is possible to invoke a theory to justify its use). What I mean is that nothing is more tedious than that endless Zen chatter that, when you uncork it, you can go on talking indefinitely about anything, interspersing the same paradoxes over and over again. But I can not imagine a Zen master slamming someone face first into the mud for for his own good, just because he felt like doing it. If this happens, it simply happens. I mean, whoever makes himself a disciple of such a master accepts by the logic of the relationship whatever comes his way.

DIALOGUE 4
...Jung

Caretti: *From Plato onwards, many philosophers have argued that theoretical, practical and aesthetic knowledge are originally linked to mythical-religious consciousness based on the symbol. How is it that although you have tried to elaborate a science of experience, you have never dealt with symbolic experience? What do you think symbolic experience is?*

Laing: We need to stop for a moment and try to clarify our terms. For example, what is our definition of 'symbol'? What should we consider our symbolic relationship to be? Is A to B, or B to C, in a symbolic relationship (as opposed to being in some other kind of relationship)? Is the experience of such a symbolic relation a symbolic experience? When we tell a tale, we are not talking about language as such, or about the phonemes of a language standing in a relationship of signifiers to signified, but we are talking about a set of signifiers organised in a particular way so as to convey a signified that is not found in them, which signified in turn refers to what we might call the signified of the signified. This is a complex system of transformations of patterns that are linked or woven together, or unified by a universal grammar of transformations. And in this symbolic field – of semantics, semiotics, semiology, communications, information – we take a special interest in the patterns of our mind, in the mental patterns that are reproduced in artistic form, in visual forms. Think of the design of a mandala, which in its interlocking circles and squares reflects a concrete experience of being at the centre of the universe. It certainly seems to be a primary way of ordering the universe and it appears to surface everywhere.

Rather than a phenomenon of cultural diffusion, it seems to be a genetically inherited mental structure, like a claw or a fruit or the number of vertebrae. It seems, therefore that we are in the field of genetic mental anatomy or mental structure. I have already spoken about all these things, taking them seriously but without going into too much detail in at least one chapter of *The Facts of Life*, where I have compared embryogems – embryological patterns of transformation in our life-cycle – with mythologems and psychologems, i.e. patterns that emerge in the fields of mythology and psychology, respectively. In these different domains, a principle of economy of pattern seems to apply.

I was especially interested in the extremely detailed parallelisms (which fascinated Jung) between our biochemical sequences and the actual embryological transformations which we all pass through in our ontogeny. For example, in Plato and elsewhere, Primeval Man is a sphere and the soul is said to have a spherical shape. Let us remember that Aristotle defined the soul as the form of the body.

And if we admit that our life-cycle begins with a zygote, then the first body form concretely assumed by our ontogenetic process is a perfect sphere. This perfect sphere is in space and must penetrate matter. It must implant itself, nest, sink into the earth, descend. The divine hero must enter the jaws of Mother Earth.

This is one of the things I am writing about right now. At the very least, it follows from the addition of the embryological series to the alchemical series, the psychological series and the mythological series, and the idea is confirmed that we have a set of structural transformations that, it is true, does not become manifest and visible in the life of all of us but which is certainly true in the life of many of us. Sometimes it expresses itself in scenarios of conduct in which people enact, that is to say experience, an act of arduous dramatisation of the eternal triangle in one of these forms or keep going in circles or, again, really find themselves or try hard to always be at the centre of their own sphere of influence, and so on. Very often these metaphors govern people's conduct and ambitions, unbeknownst to them or on an unconscious level. And, in the opinion of both Freud and Jung, it is possible to act them out. One can dream them, they can appear in visions or images, one can express them either in visual terms or as temporal sequences.

Caretti: *You have often highlighted how the 'person' is the object of your research. C.G. Jung meant by 'person' the mask of the collective psyche, a sort of compromise between the individual and society regarding "how one shows himself"; for Gabriel Marcel, on the other hand, 'person' is the reality of the individual, his true existence. Do you think your research may have been influenced by these two authors?*

Laing: I do not think I was influenced by Marcel but I certainly was influenced by Jung. I think the first thing about Jung that was a serious influence on me was his lectures on religion.

Once you have read Jung, it becomes difficult to do without his terms; for example, 'person' or 'shadow' or his psychological types. You have to be careful, because once you start using the schema, you cannot stop. You go crazy always wanting to characterise everyone in terms of a dominant function and a recessive function, of extroverted feeling, introverted intuition, and so on. Of course, *Symbols of Transformation* played a decisive role for me. It is a pioneering work for the way my work in psychiatry has been oriented ever since. It was certainly the first time I had come across the use of a mythical scenario in connection with psychological constellations or with a set of transformations in the area of real life, of actual experience. An example is the proposed myth of the hero's 'night-sea journey' first described by Frobeniuus as a concrete mythologem that corresponds to what in the jargon of clinical psychiatry is called the psychotic process.

Freud had made a completely different use of myth and *Symbols of Transformation* naturally led to his and Jung's paths diverging decisively. I have found it strange, and at the same time sad, that so many Freudians do not seem to have time to study Jung, with the result that they lose so much. Among Jungians things are different. I have met many who have assimilated Freud.

Caretti: *Are there other elements of Jungian theory that have profoundly influenced you? In particular, what do you think about the function Jung attributes to the Self?*

Laing: When speaking of theory in Jung, it must be made clear that Jungian theorising is rather unique. In Jung, it seems to me, theory reverts to its original meaning. Take, for example, the way he looks at the question of opposites. I think much of what he says – the essential line of his argument – is perfectly correct. It is difficult to fully understand Jung until one is of mature age, because the bulk of his work is about what happens in the transition to middle age and during ageing, and there is just no way to know in advance these experiences. Perhaps it is because we have two hemispheres, but the fact is that our mind seems to be structured in such a way that in the course of our life-cycle its evolution confronts us, around midlife, with a conflict in which two opposing and irreconcilable positions are at war with each other. Each side is the enemy of the other and there seems to be no room for a third position or for any possibility of reconciliation. It is either/or and this either/or does not signify a felicitous co-existence but instead a condition of extreme intrapsychic conflict. I do not know if this is true for everyone – indeed I believe that only some go through this experience. But it is a fact that a significant number of people recognise in Jung's description their own intellectual formation.

It would seem, again in a mysterious way, that not everything follows from all our intentions, all our will, our efforts, all our struggle. It is in some secret way that the torment finds its resolution. There is something alchemical about it. At the moment when this resolution occurs it becomes clear that it does not come from the two conflicting sides. In other words, it happens that one begins to feel a centre, around which his life organises itself and manifests its power. In Jungian terminology, this is the transcendental function of the Self, or the emergence of the Self, and this experience may be accompanied by a shift in the centre of gravity of existence. It seems to move from a localisation in the ego to a mysterious non-phenomenal organising centre, around which every aspect of the individual – functions, personality, energies, emotionality, etc. – and the whole world seems to order itself spontaneously, not unlike the way iron filings form a precise pattern under the influence of a magnet.

For those who have such an experience, the feeling is one of being drawn by a force outside the known, observable, predictable horizon, outside the phenomenal realm. This seems easily reconciled with Kant. Indeed, in one of his works Jung states that the Self is noumenal, and in this sense is a transcendental function, in the Kantian sense of the term.

Caretti: *Another central hypothesis of Jungian theory is the existence of 'archetypes' as primordial figures of the collective unconscious. For Jung, all human cultures and all civilisations have common symbolic roots. What do you think about this idea?*

Laing: One must remember that the Jungian notion of the archetype is very similar to the notion of the mandala in Tibetan Buddhism, or even the notion of the mantra in Hinduism. The mandala is an image of the archetype, which in itself is not an image.

There is a way of looking at the mandala, the Tibetan way, whereby it is instead a mental key that opens a state of mind. Contemplating that figure with the eyes of the mind infallibly leads us to a further state of consciousness. In Jung there is the same idea of the mandala with its centring and ordering function, that of protection and concentration of energy, and with its dynamic distribution patterns.

I think there are actually a number of forms proper to the human species that appear universally in the sense that we order our experience by representing these forms as images, or we process our input in terms of patterns that immediately (without going through images) coincide with them.

Recall *Anti-Oedipus*.[20] Again, about this spherical surface, there is a primordial form that looks like a sphere. In a two-dimensional plane, a sphere can take the form of a circle, a spiral, a circumference with us inside. In short, it is a container, a spherical container. Like the earth, it is round, and we are in its centre.

We must pay great attention to the co-ordinates of our world. Apparently, we all have some kind of spinal cord or central axis in whose terms we express what is central to our interest and other figures to indicate what is nearer or farther, what is inside or outside, what is above or below. The body is a central axis, and at this moment my right hand is my northeastern side and my left hand is my southwestern side. But if I turn around the relationship is reversed. There is no language of laterality. In fact, we feel the body, it seems, as circular and so does its whole relationship with space. Mind you, outdoor space is undoubtedly something completely different. Yet we have a sense of an axis around which we order our scheme of things and we have a tendency to place in the middle, in the centre, that which is important to us. We place it close to our heart, or within our heart and we also tend to feel it as deep rather than superficial, and so on.

It seems to me quite right to adopt a theory of archetypal or primary forms which provides an abstract guiding principle by which we can put our experience in order.

DIALOGUE 5
The Fate of the Family

Caretti: *"...the shadow of the 'family' darkens one's vision. Until one can see the 'family' in oneself, one can see neither oneself nor any family clearly."*[21] With these words in The Politics of the Family you pointed to a possible negative function of the family. Would you like to clarify this concept of the 'shadow of the family' in more detail?

Laing: It is sad to see that the family is the place of so much unhappiness for so many people today, and it is important to ask why this is so. I want to make it clear, however, that I am not proposing a global condemnation of the family, nor am I saying that the family as such has been dismissed, or that today people with common sense should avoid living within the family, or that happy families do not exist.

At the end of the day, I have derived more comfort and consolation from my family than the other way around, and I am sure that each of us knows people whose families are not plagued by dissension, narrow-mindedness, shame and the like. What we are talking about are just some families, and some situations that seem to arise in the context of the family.

In *The Politics of the Family*, I distinguish between the family as seen from the outside, as an objective social structure, and the family as the experience of its constituent persons. When we look at the ways in which individuals experience the family, we find that their experience is often traceable to one of those (perhaps archetypal) structural configurations we mentioned a moment ago. The family becomes, so to speak, an enclosure with more or less defined boundaries, which has an inside and an outside. This enclosure can be felt as benign, in which case it is an asylum, a place to return to from the world and to turn one's back on the world, or perhaps to leave for the world, but always a comfortable harbour, a refuge. In any case, a place where it is 'pleasant' to be.

In this way, the family can almost become an extension of our ego. Or one may share one's identity with other family members, and in this case we have the situation described by Mary Barnes[22] as an undifferentiated family ego. Once such a situation has arisen, one easily finds oneself identifying one's ontological security with one's ego, and naturally this ego will have to defend itself. Again, as Lacan points out, this enterprise of supporting, preserving and possibly expanding one's ego becomes a normalised paranoid enterprise. And the same can happen if one identifies with the family, which then becomes a fortress. Or, better, a castle with a moat around it and a drawbridge, and one may suffer if the bridge is lowered, as can occasionally happen. In this case, the family is always subject to the threat of disenchantment or of an attack brought by external forces felt to be enemies.

Or the family can be perceived as an evil enclosure, and then it becomes a prison. In this case, the enterprise becomes one of getting out of the family, but it becomes a trap. A situation is created that makes us hostile and which we feel is suffocating because of the narrowness of its boundaries, and as such depriving us of our freedom.

Thus the fantasy of the family, the family as a fantasised system of relationships projected onto the family itself, or even onto any social whole, obscures to our eyes – not unlike any other unacknowledged fantasy, benign or hostile – the real situation. I believe that what the psychoanalytical terminology defines as a fantasy should be considered as a natural and ineradicable aspect of our minds. And I would not dream of saying that we must abolish the fantasy, any more than I would say that we must abolish dreams or imagination. We must, however, free our minds from that possible epistemological error that consists in confusing the fantasy with what the phantom itself is projected onto. This is another example of the social illusion. Not that it is an impenetrable illusion. The point is not that the shadows on the cave wall are in themselves taken as shadows, illusions. Shadows only become illusions if we exchange them for the essence. Briefly, the illusion is not the shadow. The illusion is the error of confusing the shadow with that of which the shadow is a shadow.

Another feature of this aspect of the family is that it is the place where most of us originally learn our social skills, including language, how to move, what we can touch or say, or what noises we are allowed to make (what kind of noises and how loud, when, with whom and where). The most particular details of our social being take shape largely in our relationships with other family members, and, in general, the child everywhere in Europe lives the first years of his or her life almost completely surrounded by family members. In this respect, the period of childhood has unique characteristics, and it is necessary to examine how and how much is transmitted or imparted or learned or copied in those crucial early years.

In *The Politics of the Family* and elsewhere I draw attention to a fact which, I believe, anyone who has worked in the area of the family will admit is present in some, though not all, families. It is this: sometimes the members of a family seem to have fallen into reciprocal relationships with one another which in some ways resemble hypnotic relationships. In a hypnotic relationship one can experience virtually anything as real simply because things are described to one in the context of the hypnotic relationship. In other words, I believe what you say because you have told me so; things are so because you say so; things are so because I tell you they are so; and why this is right or wrong, or why things are the way they are, is why I say they are, no matter whether explicitly or implicitly.

In hypnosis, for example, the hypnotised person may be told that he is going to sip a first-rate dry sherry. He is then given an ordinary drink and he will taste it in his mouth and swallow it, and it will be a first-rate dry sherry. But if you put the same material in the mouth of the same person who has come out of hypnotic sleep, he may find it absolutely disgusting. This happened to me under hypnosis. Hypnotic suggestion is capable of generating an experience that is the exact opposite of the real thing. And the situation becomes extremely problematic if even our taste, our touch, our identity, our body image and, again, what we hear with our own ears, what we see with our own eyes, is susceptible to such complete modification as to create the illusion of something that is not present, the illusion that there is something that is not there, to create, in short, the impression that things are completely different from what they are.

Anyone (whether he is in difficulty or not) who really wants to engage in the enterprise of purifying his mind will come to terms with 'how' and 'how much' the idea he has of anything is what it is because someone has told him that this is how it is. Even Kierkegaard, perhaps ironically and perhaps seriously, perhaps joking and perhaps not, once asked himself why he believed in God and answered, "Because my father told me so".

For many children, at least in my country, one of life's great epistemological crises (crises of trust and belief) is linked to Santa Claus. I remember that when, after much pressure, my parents ended up telling me the truth (I was five years old), I had a devastating feeling of having been deceived. As great as it might have been, my gratitude to them (now discovered to be the real Santa Claus) was for years completely eclipsed by the feeling of having been wronged, since they had (so it seemed to me) systematically deceived me.

A lady told me about a little girl who at the age of seven still believed in fairies. Her mother talked to her about fairies all the time, and she was in an intimate relationship with the fairies and the fairy world. Once they were spending the winter in a remote country place and when the weather turned very cold, the child, who was now seven-and-a-half-years-old, became very worried that the fairies would catch cold. And she knitted several dozen little dresses, which she placed by her bed one night for the fairies to collect. The mother was so moved by this that she collected the clothes and left a little fairy doll beside her daughter's bed. The girl was overjoyed that the fairies had come and taken her present. Well, this illusion – which is not simply a single event in the little girl's belief system but is deeply interwoven with what is true and what is not; with what one believes and trusts; with what one is told and how one can believe what one believes; interwoven with whom one believes and what one trusts about what one hears – is perhaps a benign illusion. Yet we feel that the little girl, as she grows up, will have to, in one way or another, go through a major crisis which will be very tormenting for the mother as well as for the daughter and will affect the girl's entire sense of reality for the rest of her life.

This is the kind of thing that matters deep down. Apart, of course, from anything to do with incest (why cannot the mother sleep with her son, the father with his daughter, the brother with his sister; the answers we give our children on these subjects when we give them answers and whatever they may be (looks, gestures or explicit assertions)) always intrigue the child a great deal, and they too forcefully enter into the deep determination of the warp and woof of the idea that one originally had of things. If one abandons such an idea, one has to question the whole nexus of familiar events in which (and from which) it has primarily taken shape.

Remember Sartre. His reading of the Freudian project is largely an attempt to demystify through method any and all mystifications in which one may find oneself imprisoned regarding one's family relationships. To attribute a certain degree of importance to the family is not to make it the dominant factor, but simply to acknowledge its presence and to try to understand its contribution to our lives.

Caretti: *Some have seen in your theories of the family system a stance against the family, a kind of eulogy of its disappearance. What do you think?*

Laing: To the extent that I can demystify myself, I do not recognise in what I have said or written the presence of any ideological position regarding the family. My view of families is that they are, as the family system, the best social group known to me. I detest the idea of the dissolution of the family system of couples, as, for example, is happening in America. A few months ago, American sociologists told me about a new problem facing American courts in divorce matters. It used to be the rule that when two spouses separated, a battle would ensue because both wanted custody of the children. Today, however, courts are increasingly faced with a situation where neither spouse wants custody of the children, and judges have to resolve the very delicate issue of what to do with them, whom to give them to. Parents seem to be losing the sense of connection between themselves and their children, and I find this very sad.

I have also been told that middle-class family clubs have sprung up in California under the banner of incest. It is probably the last stop on the way for 'swingers'. They got married, had kids and now they are coming to the family orgy, to an understanding among families about a group gang-bang, indiscriminately gathering together members of two or three family groups – husbands and wives, fathers and mothers, sons and daughters, brothers and sisters. However, I do not like this. On the one hand, I tend to see in this phenomenon a sort of sociological adaptation to the extreme position of the uprooted family, in which there are only two generations or maybe only one (this is the case for the nuclear couple), and which is in a condition of a very serious anthropological anomaly, namely, just two people, each responsible to the other for the sole satisfaction of its emotional, sexual, economic and physical needs. And even if there are children, one or both parents spend most of the day away from home at work. In the best of cases, the children stay with the mother alone. The father is away for an enormous amount of time and his figure oscillates, as Margaret Mead observed, between that of a tired family man in the office and a tired businessman at home. Neither parent is capable of rest, and each pounces on the partner to wring out the emotional and sexual comfort that both are too exhausted to give. And this is the terrible picture that emerges when the nuclear family loses its vitality, as happens so often. Just look at the frequency of divorce in Western America. If I am not mistaken, over fifty percent of couples who marry end up divorcing.

The forms of marriage and the family, the very idea of marriage itself, are today under great pressure and tension, and are going through a phase of transition. If we read the novelists of the nineteenth century or even of our own century, we see that very few of them praise the family. I do not want to fall into an idealisation of the good old days, with its marriages that resulted in the buying and selling of women (think Flaubert), in essence, as Shaw says, not much better than legalised prostitution. There is no need to idealise the abject legal and economic position created for women in this kind of family system, a ruthless and cynical system characterised by patriarchal hierarchy.

Other family systems, which have developed outside the Western world, seem to me to be too closely linked to their cultural contexts to be easily transplanted. And yet, without wishing to idealise or project a spectral ideal onto the family or confuse the real family with the spectral family, I retain — or so it seems to me — the sense of a family ideal and try to make it operative in my own family life. Personally, I have not turned my back on the family. On the contrary, I say that if a family works well, if the members of the couple are happy to be together, if they enjoy each other, if they like and love each other, despite all the inevitable ups and downs and all the difficulties, then I cannot imagine a better environment in which to raise a child. So I do not like the idea of seeing the family as a system disappearing or falling apart.

Caretti: *Do you mean that the family is disappearing?*

Laing: It is disappearing in the form we have known it. On the West Coast of America it is crumbling and we cannot say whether this is a harbinger of what will happen in Europe. It could be a localised collapse, a feature of the way of life in that region, which is after all extremely different from ours. I have picked up (I do not remember where) what seems to me to be an excellent observation about the American scene: there, time and space are in a completely different relationship than here. In America, space has expanded and time has contracted, so that there are enormous spaces travelled at very high speeds. You do not think twice about driving one hundred miles for a drink. On the other hand, the whole architectonic cycle has been compressed into about twenty years. It is as though a twenty-year-old house is turned into a museum piece. Time has contracted, space has expanded, with the result that one is frantically on the move all the time without having a minute to spare. It is as though time were reset to zero.

Travelling around America, as I have done many times, and living in hotels, I have witnessed the astonishing spectacle offered by an American hotel at breakfast time: the large dining room is packed with businessmen, almost all with their eyes on the newspaper, while fifty-year-old waitresses with their white or pinkish hair, always curled, in short skirts, tennis shoes and aprons, serve them their eggs cooked for two to three minutes. All these men spend an enormous amount of their time away from home. I do not know the exact figures now, but it is many times more time than any other group of men. These are people who spend ten times more time on the road than anyone else on the face of the earth. And where are the wives and children of all these men? In Europe we are much more attached to the home.

The farther south you go, the more you realise that not only women and children but also men live in families and spend a large part of their time at home. Sure, in a small Italian town, the men will all be at the café in the square (where the women do not go), but their homes are around the corner and not hundreds of miles away on the highway.

Caretti: *What is the place you give to love in interpersonal relationships?*

Laing: The English word 'love' has two completely different meanings. On the one hand it is used to designate Christian or Buddhist charity, or any other form of charity. In the trinity of faith, hope and charity, the last is the greatest virtue.

You can have faith and hope too, but without charity, faith and hope will be empty. In this sense, to love is to see the essence of the other as the other is. The definition comes from St. Thomas Aquinas. But it does not matter that it is made explicit; this is still the essence of the matter. In this sense, I would say love is almost synonymous with knowing. And it certainly implies knowing. I do not see how one can love anything without knowing what it is that one loves. Nor do I see how, if we are talking about interpersonal knowledge, we can know another person if we do not let him or her be for us as he or she is in himself or herself; that is to say, if we hanker after him or her in an instrumental way for purposes of manipulation, modification, control or power. Of course, I am talking about the other as a person. I mean, here it is not about the instrumental knowledge that is indispensable to a surgeon, say, who has to remove an appendix. I am not asking the surgeon to take an interest in me. I just want him to remove my appendix, as quickly, as efficiently, as cheaply and as painlessly as possible. And that is it.

Love, to love…we take love in relation to the whole cosmos: a loving relationship, a friendly relationship. Let us take the case of someone who says that he is bound by friendship to humanity. Well, to be able to say something like that seems to me very nice. This man harbours no rancour, no malice, no anxiety over revenge, no feelings of spite, bitterness or envy. Nor does he look at others or at the world in a ruthlessly cynical way, seeing in them only an opportunity for actions to enhance his personal (and illusory) power, prestige, status, self-love or whatever. Nor, in such a man, is it a question of forgiveness of offences or guilt. In this kind of love there is no guilt or offence.

The other meaning of the English word 'love' is desire in a broad sense, not necessarily sexual desire, but any desire. I love you means I want you, I desire you. The trouble with men and women is that they want different things: men want women, women want men. Desire…if I may venture a generalisation, I would say that when desire appears, very often love seems to fly out the window. If and to the extent that what animates me is desire not tempered by love, I have no particular interest in the person I desire, since what matters to me is the satisfaction of my desire. If I aspire to renew my satisfaction, it is obvious that I want the gratification of the object that satisfies my desire. If whom I desire is to be flattered, clearly I need a flatterer, and I cannot afford to destroy the object of my desire. Suppose

I have a woman who is economically dependent. Suppose also that I do not want other people to satisfy their desire with the same object, which I intend to reserve exclusively for myself. Well, I will have no problem, if I have enough money, to treat this woman with great generosity and extravagance so that she is happy and remains attractive and amiable, and so on.

I remember once when my wife was ill and the doctor who examined her on the way out said to me, "Take good care of your wife; of all your tools, she is, of course, the most important piece." What I am trying to make clear is that in terms of need and desire there is a way of caring for the object of love which is very much like the way a gunman cares for his revolver, or a cowboy cares for his horse. What drives the gunman or the cowboy is the utility that the object of love has for them. So this form of solicitude, concern, handling and the like may seem very similar to the solicitude, care, regard and appreciation proper to love, but it is far removed from it. In fact, it goes in exactly the opposite direction.

One may wonder if it is possible to be animated by a conscious desire and, at the same time, to love, if the two things are not in fact mutually incompatible. And certainly in all monastic orders, monks, celibates make a specific effort to extinguish desire, to erase it, to uproot it. As the Buddhists say, it is not just a matter of cutting down the tree. One has to tear out the roots to the deepest and most remote fibres and expel from one's heart absolutely all desire so that, purified, the heart and mind can welcome the radiance of love, whose splendour desire would tarnish like clouds do the splendour of the sun.

I believe I am enough a man of the Western world (though not in the cynical sense) for it to sound improper to say that I have arrived at such reconciliation or that this reconciliation has in any case occurred in my life. But I have not lost the sense of its possibility and I have not convinced myself that it is a priori impossible to achieve it. On the contrary, one can imagine that if love and desire merge with complete reciprocity and at the same time, then the concrete possibility of a perfect marriage is created. And I think we should at least aim for perfection in everything we say and do.

DIALOGUE 6
Family and Schizophrenia

Caretti: *From love we return to the family. Why has it become a central theme in your research?*

Laing: I would like to distinguish my approach to the study of families from what one might call in its various forms ideological familism, and by which, to give an example, Deleuze and Guattari in their *Anti-Oedipus* find me somewhat influenced. I came to study families – in other words, our society – in a very simple way. I began by being inspired by the view that schizophrenia is not exclusively something *in* a person. Instead, the attribution of schizophrenia arises in the context of, and is often provoked by, a particular disjunctive pattern of interpersonal relationships. It then dawned on me that virtually all observations of so-called schizophrenics take place within the walls of the psychiatric clinic. I became increasingly aware (although not as explicitly as Foucault shows himself to be in his later writings) that the way of seeing and knowing, which is an integral and essential part of the European clinic as an institution, involves a certain way of looking at the other, and that it is precisely that way of looking at the other that seems to contribute, on the one hand, to driving him crazy and, on the other, to making him seen by others as insane. But it became perfectly clear to me that if one wanted to understand something of these schizophrenics, there was no point in studying them in the hospital. Of course, they were people who had come to the hospital as a result of an expulsion from a system of communication, of interaction, in short, a social group that existed outside the hospital. I began to read the literature on what actually happened there and I realised that there is practically nothing, even with regard to the work of observing families, that derives from the clinical context. At that time it all boiled down to Lidz's research on families, a lot of the work that was done at Yale and the National Institute for Mental Health in Washington, and a few other things. Then there was the concept of the schizophrenogenic mother.

So I began to look around and to look at what was going on outside the context of the clinic. I got involved in the study of families, but I could just as well have gotten involved in the study of workplaces, schools, and generally where there is any kind of human grouping. But it is true that in reality it is the nuclear family that in practice turns out to be the immediately relevant group in the life of each of us. I could have studied institutionalised children, people brought up in institutions and not in families. In any case, there seemed to be an amount of mystification, confusion and conflict that lent itself very well to being recorded on tape and reproduced in a text that was itself open to analysis and comment. I have always been keen to emphasise that I have never put forward the hypothesis that the family, or perhaps society, causes schizophrenia. Instead, I have said that schizophrenia, assuming the term has any meaning (often extended to functional psychosis), is a medical diagnosis. It is a medical diagnosis that makes its appearance only when a doctor in the role of psychiatrist looks at another person and sees in his conduct (as expressed above all in his physical behaviour in his words and actions) the manifestations of some organic pathological process.

Now, there is not the slightest doubt that schizophrenia is in fact a hypothesis, and precisely the following hypothesis, that such conduct of the other is the manifestation of an organic pathological process. So far no one has identified this process, and most of those diagnosed as schizophrenic are, in the ordinary sense of the term, in perfect physical health. That such an organic pathological process taking place at the microbiological, cellular level does indeed exist is possible. The point, however, is that it has not yet been discovered. What is more, if you have not discovered any organic pathological process, I can say that you have not proved the existence of such an organic pathological process. In other words, the medical diagnosis of schizophrenia coincides with the hypothesis that such a process is there waiting to be discovered. Very well, I recognise that this is a perfectly valid hypothesis. It is not a hypothesis that I am personally interested in investigating, because I am neither a biochemist nor a pathologist. But as a hypothesis it is entirely legitimate and feasible. No argument about that. All I am saying is that it is not yet a fact but only, precisely, a hypothesis. Some may think that it is a hypothesis whose plausibility is almost introduced by intuition, but a hypothesis remains such until it has been confirmed.

In my opinion, genetic and demographic studies do not especially testify to the plausibility of this hypothesis since their findings can be interpreted in a variety of ways. It is only in the last few years, for example in Denmark, that an adequate census of the entire population has been carried out, so that it is actually possible to undertake scientifically respectable genetic studies. Moreover, given certain transformations in the organic state of such an individual, it does not follow that the organic is not part of the social. There is a biochemistry of fear. Agreed, but it is nevertheless very simplistic to say "I am frightened because there is adrenalin circulating in my blood" or something like that. One could just as well say that there is adrenaline circulating in my blood because I am frightened. In any case, if I am frightened, I am frightened by other people; that is, my fear is part of a social situation. A social situation can therefore affect my physical being, my organism, my chemistry and the functioning of my nervous system. If I get a piece of information that makes me stagger, it can happen that my movements become uncoordinated and I stagger. I have seen people stagger when they have been told a certain thing. So it is clear that in this way the information actually influences our physiology. If there is a chemistry of terror, there is also a chemistry of chronic despair – there is indeed a chemistry of everything. So we cannot assess these things properly until scientists have developed an authentic social chemistry, or until chemical data are studied in social situations so that we are able to discern which social variables induce which correlative modifications in the chemical variables of our bodies. In conclusion, anyone who wants to adopt the hypothesis that a certain behaviour depends on an organic pathological process and to act accordingly is perfectly entitled to do so, but I repeat that this process has not yet been discovered. As for me, all I can do is to look at the intelligibility of this conduct in relation to myself and in relation to other persons, and thus undertake to investigate further what is in each individual case the nature of that intelligibility.

In practice, for many psychiatrists the schizophrenic is *ipso facto* such simply because the way he behaves is unintelligible. I know, however, that there are people (certainly a minority) who (I do not know why) do not find it too difficult to make out the intelligibility of a series of behaviours generally considered to be unintelligible. And once one begins to understand, the fact that such intelligibility is not noticed seems increasingly strange. One is then led to think that either psychiatrists deny what they see, or they look in a particular way that precludes them from seeing. This is illustrated in *The Divided Self* by the ambiguous figure consisting of two lines facing each other. If you look at this figure in a certain way you will see a vase and if you continue to study vases you will never see the two human profiles facing each other. So I began to suppose that it was nothing but cynical superficiality, dull inattention or stupidity. For example, you are in a room with someone who is scared stiff. Now, you do not see this fear, nor can you imagine why this person should be scared to death – and *then* you see someone suffering from catatonic schizophrenia. And that is all you can see, you cannot even see the person behind the patient. In any case, I found myself increasingly involved in what we might call the microsociology of the person-to-person, body-to-body relationship, of the interaction between members of a couple, between parents and children, or between any group of people. In interpersonal relationships, an extreme case of disjunction (rather than conjunction) occurs when a person begins to be seen on the hypothesis that he or she is freaking out, that what he or she is trying to communicate has no meaning, is indeed devoid of any sense or rationality, is, in short, unintelligible.

Personally, I have no difficulty, in most cases, in discerning intelligibility and rationality and meaning, and so on. By this I do not mean that I agree with the person as having been diagnosed as psychotic or, let us say, as insane. I can very well feel that the guy is insane. He may be perplexed, bewildered, confused, mystified. He may be shattered, scattered. He may not feel that there are human beings around him or that he is alive. He may even not feel that he has been born or that he is in this world. He may hear things that I do not hear, or see things that I do not see; or he may not see or hear much of what I see and hear. The minds of such people are sometimes in a desperate state of confusion and disorder. Their universe is an inextricable mess. Yet, when we look at the concrete, personal, immediate interactions of their social microcosm and examine the system of communication that operates there, the fact that they are in such a mess becomes much more understandable.

Considering the context in which they live, that confusion is an internalisation of that context and a response to it. This is what we all do. We all assimilate the context, we welcome it into ourselves, so to speak, and we incorporate it into our relationship with ourselves. We derive from it something like a system of relations in which and for which we subsist, and we then re-project this system externally onto the system around us, which we interpret accordingly. This means the process of internalisation, and then externalisation of what has been internalised, necessarily involves some transformations.

Caretti: *In our civilisation, the psychological necessity of the relationship with the 'father' (be it the real or symbolic father) is a central aspect of the collective consciousness. In* The Politics of the Family, *however, the role of the father, with the associated problem of authority and its sexual characterisation, is almost completely absent from the framework of family interrelations you propose.*

Laing: That is true. But the fact is that my book is by no means intended to be a systematic and exhaustive theoretical exposition of the politics of the family. It limits itself to isolating certain themes, completely leaving out some of the most difficult ones, such as the whole problem of sexuality as such, and also the authority of the father and mother and all that is summed up in the Oedipal schema.

In *The Politics of the Family*, authority is treated in terms of the concept of injunction, the force of which – that is, the power or effectiveness or ability of an injunction to be obeyed – depends on the authority of the injunction itself. I am not sure that there is not a tautology here. It depends on the location, in terms of power, of the foundation of the injunction in social space. If, say, a sister says something to an older brother, her words have a completely different weight than if they came from a father in full authority. In a great many of the families I studied, there was no consensus about who held authority or about the form of authority. The authority claimed by one person could be undermined by another. The father tried to lay down the law and the mother might sabotage it, while denying what she was doing (or vice versa). Or the two parents had diametrically opposed representations of the child. Suppose A and B disagree diametrically about the same person, C, of whom they have mutually reversed images. They do not admit the disagreement, they do not open up to each other and let it come to light. Thus, two persons have completely different images of the identity of a third person. A and B disagree about who C is, and conceal this disagreement from C. As a result, C has the tormenting sense of not knowing who or what he or she is. When C turns to A or B, they tell him who he or she really is, pretending to agree, or perhaps ignoring that they do not agree. It is a situation we often find with adopted children or when a woman claims that the child is her husband's (so she tells both of them) but it is not true. So, one day, for example, the son starts to say "You are not my father". I have a very vivid memory of such a case. A woman brought her seventeen-year-old son to me and said he was becoming psychotic because he did not treat his father as such. But later she confided to me (in absolute secrecy, of course, without the child knowing) that the boy was not her husband's child. She had never told her husband about this and would have preferred to see her son committed to a psychiatric hospital as a psychotic rather than admit the truth or try to understand that admitting the truth could be very useful after all.

To return to the question of authority, it is very difficult to take a generalisation such as Nietzsche's utterance "God is dead" and apply it to the empirical study of a family. But, as Lacan says, it is certain that the place of the father is often left empty. It is not occupied by the man who is called the father, nor does it seem to be occupied by anyone else. In fact, the place is purely and simply empty. There is a vacancy for a male authority, but the authority that actually exists (when it does exist) is often not what is properly called an authority. It is terror, it is mere power, brute force, which does not arouse the slightest respect but only fear.

The whole question of the so-called sexual characterisation (male or female) of the deeper program of injunctions presents itself to feminists as a very complex matter. I am going to use this expression for now – program, programming, no matter whether it is characterised as masculine or feminine – because I believe that this goes back largely to before birth. Looking at things from the point of view of what later becomes a sexually characterised injunction, it is not clear whether the womb or the maternal body as experienced from within is not assimilated in some respects to something masculine. For example, I have collected indications from both men and women that go in this direction. I am thinking in particular of a woman who told me: "I need an authority that makes me feel pain. I need to feel a man around me, I mean not a man who is *here*, but a man who in a way surrounds and contains me. I need to feel a certain pressure from him that makes me emerge from myself." It is as if this woman is saying that she is a foetus in the uterine space, contained by this space, and that it is necessary for this uterus to contract (or for an authority to press on her) in order for her to be ejected out. As you see, the schema of the scenario takes the form of the intrauterine situation, and of being born as being pushed out by a pressure. But what I want to point out is that the woman identifies this condition, which we can say is 'uterine' as male.

There are similar original structures, analogous to this being surrounded and contained. One may feel comfortable being contained by a social form or one may feel compressed and perhaps completely crushed. A man may feel that the sense of authority crushes him, suffocates him or even annihilates him. But the point is that there is a plurality of patterns and that is one of the things I am now trying to work out.

The Oedipal schema seems to be a special case of a triangular relationship – whose terms are, again, felt as masculine or feminine – between A, B and C (assuming that this triangle sums up the meaning of the Oedipus schema). I think that the Freudian interpretation of the Oedipus myth is, in the words of Lévi-Strauss, "itself one of the transformations of the whole". It is not a metalevel; it is not looking at a set of transformations of that triangle. Let me explain further. There is A, B and C. A and B have a relationship and C is the third. C wants to take the place of A in relation to B, or the place of B in relation to A. C therefore wishes to interfere in the relationship between A and B. C wishes to form a relationship with B and exclude A, or to form a relationship with A and exclude

B. Well, this allows for a certain number of transformations, of which the Freudian interpretation is only one of many possible. In the same way, A is the mother, B is the father and C is Oedipus. Oedipus (as C) wishes to annihilate B and replace him in his relationship with A. But this does not end the game. It is but one move, a set of moves in the game. But things could just as well go differently or take one direction or the other. I do not believe, in short, that the Freudian account is, so to speak, a primary model. It is only one of the possible transformations of the whole. But there is more. The Freudian version of the Oedipus story is, from the point of view of a mythologist or anthropologist, scandalous, if only because Jocasta was the bride of Laius, and Laius is one of the traditional mythical introducers of homosexuality into Greece. In other words, it is an absolutely atypical situation.

I am not even convinced that the movement of our libido must necessarily fixate on these originary 'objects'. I say not necessarily, although sometimes it certainly does happen. I agree with Deleuze and Guattari when they say that Oedipus, fixated on, riveted to this originary triangle, does not represent the way our spirit acts when it is uncorrupted and unafraid. In other words, libido is expansive. We want to get out, to go away, and if we seek the strange, the new, the different, the adventure, it is not because we are fleeing from our mother. If, however, we are injured in our sortie, or if we are already frightened before we make a move, then it may be that, like a sick and frightened animal, we perversely draw back, to take refuge in the suffocating libidinal warmth of our mothers and fathers. I think this is a perversion. That is, I am convinced that what Freud proposed as a canonical scheme, as a normative model, is in fact a special case of a perverse relationship.

Caretti: *I agree with you when you criticise this conception of the unconscious as perverse. However Jacques Lacan, as you know, maintains that the recognition of the "name of the father" allows the subject to overcome the mirror phase. In other words, for Lacan, as for most Freudians, it is through symbolic castration that one arrives at psychological maturity and genitality. Do you agree with this? Or is your conception of the superego different?*

Laing: It seems to me that it is in *The Ego and the Id* that Freud puts forward the idea that one of the essential layers of the process of internalisation of the superego is the internalisation of what he calls the "primal scene". This is what we were talking about a moment ago. We have A, B and C and the internalisation of this relationship, with C's destructive hatred projected onto it and then turned against the self or the ego. I do not know who could reject the proposition that there is a universal human structure – which I think it is correct to describe as archetypal – which must be filled with some content. There is, so to speak, a 'place' within us whose mental function consists of approving and disapproving, compensating and punishing, absolving from guilt and condemning. Well, according to Freud, the energy of this superego is above all concentrated in the area we were speaking of and it emanates from there. If we compare different languages – on the one hand, say, Lacan's algorithms and on the other the analogies Freud establishes between the metapsychological apparatus and a microscope or a telescope – numerous critical observations show up. I have never been able to correlate Lacan's concepts with Freud's, to identify in the Lacanian system precise correspondences with the Freudian structures of ego, superego, etc. The "name of the father" is not really the superego, nor does it correspond exactly to any other element of Freudian metapsychology. So if we talk about the superego and its relation to castration, and then bring up the name of the father and the like, it is as if we start out speaking Russian and suddenly introduce Arabic and Chinese terms that do not belong to the same discourse. I do not believe that they mesh with the former.

Take the term 'castration'. Well, even in Freud it is not simply the threat of castration in its historical, concrete sense but instead is in essence a phylogenetically inherited propensity to feel that our physical genitality, in relation to our sexuality, will be taken away from us by our father. What seems to be at stake here, then, as with the Freudian version of the Oedipus myth, is a particular example of a set of possible transformations that have to do with the limitations of our power, that is, the disempowerment of our being perhaps down to the zero level.

Any expansion of our territory, of our existence and presence in the world, encounters limitations posed by counter-presences and in particular by our co-existence with other people. Without falling into the position that Deleuze and Guattari accuse familism of, these other persons must be the 'originary others'. If we speak in terms of concrete historical contingency, this horizon takes on formidable importance and necessarily includes our oldest vital experiences. There are the others, there are brothers and sisters, and there are others outside our immediate circle, all in a dynamic system of counterweights, of actions and feedbacks, that undergoes constant adjustments. We have to achieve this co-existence among ourselves: the place we recognise for others, the place others recognise for themselves and the place they recognise for us, with all the problems associated with the different areas of power, the efforts to get what we want, the impossibility of getting what we want and under what conditions, and so on.

Within this horizon lies the "fraternity terror" of which Sartre speaks in the *Critique of Dialectical Reason*. Also that the threat our fellow man brings against us may be arbitrary or perhaps completely absurd. It may be consistent, it may represent what will happen to us if we do not do what is expected of us or it may simply crash down on us. All our representations of what may happen to us on Earth and to God in heaven are of necessity deeply influenced by our social experience. I am not prepared to accept the idea that the whole plot of our mythical metaphors is nothing more than a translation of the theme of castration in terms of myth. I do not think it is castration in its specific and literal sense that is at stake. It is torture, it is crucifixion, it is being torn apart, dismembered, scourged. It is all the terrible things we imagine could be done to us, accompanied by all the reasons we give for them, since they have in a sense already happened and the punishment must correspond to a fault. Let us bear in mind that all states of dismemberment, or of being crucified or disfigured, or reduced to dust or in all imaginable ways destroyed completely or partially by others, are on the one hand attributed to what will become of us in a life beyond death, but on the other hand thought of as possible in this life itself, since everything has happened to someone, and it is therefore not impossible that it should happen to us within the range of our existence. Freud himself in *The Interpretation of Dreams* attributes these fantasies about Doomsday and the afterlife to perhaps even prenatal experiences, but he never introduces this aspect into his notion of the Oedipus complex and the castration complex. In short, what I am saying is that the notion of castration must be extended to this set of transformations, of which castration proper is only a particular case. I do not see any reason to confine it to what happens at four or three years of age. One can go back as far as the loss of the breast, the cutting of the umbilical cord. In other words, the sense of being cut off or of losing part of one's self is another aspect of castration. In Freud we find two different positions: first, castration is presented as a historically real threat, and, second, as a retrospective fantasy based on the projection we make onto the other of what we would like to do to him. That is, Freud thought of the father as re-internalised in terms of the threat of castration because this is precisely what the son wants to do to the father. We should construct a multidimensional diagram capable of highlighting all the different possibilities of the theme of castration: castration as an originary threat or as the product of a plurality of possible operations. In the latter case castration becomes, independent of the existence of any originary threat, a phantom generated by entirely implicit and never explicit transpersonal operations, as well as a physical metaphor for the general co-existence of us with the other in its terrifying aspect of man as enemy and traitor of man.

Caretti: *Our civilisation has replaced the rite with the spectacle, the sorcerer with the priest. The impossibility of ritualising emotional life or individual transformations – this lack of freedom to represent oneself out in the open – is probably one of the reasons for many existential problems. Do you not think that schizophrenia could be a failed ritual?*

Laing: Yes and no. I can refer to an essay I wrote in 1966.[23] Using the term 'ritual' in its anthropological as well as its theological sense, I proposed at that time the idea that certain conduct of the kind we call schizophrenic might be seen as para-ritual or meta-ritual or as the deritualisation of our ordinary rituals. Anthropologists find it very difficult to follow psychoanalysts when they speak of obsessive ritual behaviour, because obsessive behaviour, in what we call its ritualised habits, is the exact opposite of what ritual is for the anthropologist, in whose eyes everything that is ritual necessarily has a social character. In the case of obsessive behaviour, we can perhaps speak of a de-ritualisation or de-socialisation on both sides, in the sense that one person is 'out of it' in that he gesticulates and speaks in a way different from the usual, and others find it difficult or impossible to have a conversation with him. It has been suggested that this state of affairs occurs in our Western societies partly because we do not have consistent social rituals in the current anthropological sense. Or, if there are any, we do not know how to recognise them. In any case, the fact is that they remain obscure and seem to have disappeared. Now, if on the one hand this seems very plausible, on the other hand

I find it very difficult to see how this hypothesis can be substantiated.

People who live in other societies, such as India or Ceylon, or anthropologists who have conducted field research in undeveloped tribal communities with considerable ritual behaviour (in Africa, Morocco and Brazil), tell me that in these societies characterised by a strong presence of the ceremonial, there are people who in one way or another remain outside it and who seem to be the equivalent of our schizophrenics. What I mean is that it seems possible to establish some kind of parallel between the situation of these 'ex-communicants', between these 'islands of communicative non-reciprocity' and the condition of the schizophrenic in the West. Even in a deeply ritualised society, such as traditional Islamic Morocco, there are insane people in the mosques. There is always a rite and there are always certain people who stay out of it. They are considered insane. Now, what I want to stress is that in these African or Brazilian societies the cause of this social dislocation is seen differently than in ours. Far from attributing this state of affairs to a disease, to a pathological process going on in the body of that particular person, they think that it is his karma; that this person is possessed; that a god or a spirit is tormenting him; that he has become the battleground of certain demons; that it is a punishment for some wicked crime committed in a previous life; and so on. This phenomenon of social dislocation occurs not only in our deritualised societies but also in highly ritualised ones. This is why I am not very convinced by the general thesis that traces schizophrenia in whole or in part to deritualisation.

If we want to avoid ideology and stick to the concrete, we have to turn to those recent studies that deal with what happens when a person dies. Statistical data show a strong correlation between schizophrenia and the death of a parent or the separation of parents. This is not only during childhood but also around the age of fifteen or sixteen, an age that is generally said to be quite vulnerable. In short, the statistical material tells us that a majority of people diagnosed as schizophrenic lost a parent or were separated from their parents before the age of sixteen. Now, a comparison with the material offered by anthropological and ethnological studies on mourning behaviour shows that we – and this is a trait that distinguishes us – suppress our tears and become impassive. Certainly not in Italy, but in this country you have to keep your eyes dry at funerals. No one is tearing their clothes or pulling their hair out or moaning or groaning, but everyone is holding their breath. No hymns are sung together, there is no explicit sharing of feelings and, in the face of this absence, some people today speak of a virtually apathetic reaction, of an inability to mourn.

This inability should not be understood so much as a literal inability to grieve effectively as a lack of freedom to express mourning, which includes the freedom to share one's pain with others, so that this pain is not reduced to something miserable and lonely. Traditionally, mourning is, in many ways, an occasion for social gratification and strengthening the bonds between those left behind. Mourning brings people together instead of leaving alone (isolating) in his lonely room, afraid to go out into the street and face people, the person who has suffered the loss. In the past you went out into the street, but you wore black for a long time, that is, you wore a ritual marker. And this, far from excluding you, gave you a specific place among others, actually gave you a socially effective role to play. All this has almost completely disappeared today. It seems clear that for some more than for others, this results in increased tension. In short, there are those who find it difficult to overcome these emotional catastrophes without relying on ritual occasions that allow them to share the catastrophes with other people within a given formal context.

DIALOGUE 7
Between 'Journey' And Madness

Caretti: *The originality of your work has highlighted in contemporary psychology the possibility of going beyond the principle of normality/madness and considering 'abnormality' as an integral aspect of overall human experience. Do you think it is possible to hypothesise a condition of normality/madness also for the therapist?*

Laing: We cannot speak so simplistically about normality or madness in someone. It must first be said that in both normality and madness there is, at least to a certain extent, a relationship with the world, a way of being in the world and of being with others that can never be totally extrapolated from their relationship with us. So I would not put it in terms of wondering whether there is normality or madness in the therapist. As Tillich says, there are ontological possibilities for everyone. The last time I saw him, shortly before he died, I spoke to him about this and he explained to me that we are faced with non-being in the form of metaphysical, biological and moral non-being: on the one hand, the annihilation of ourselves in the physical sense, on the other hand, the annihilation of ourselves in terms of futility, of the absence of any meaning, of a feeling of zero value, that is, of not having morally a speck of goodness.

It seems to me that there is a fourth possibility to be considered alongside these three and that is the possibility of the loss of coherence; that is, the loss of a coherent relationship with a coherent world (where this relationship must be characterised by cultural consonance, since coherence must be reciprocal). One can maintain a kind of one-way coherence, not shared with anyone else; in other words, a paranoid coherence, a paranoid organisation or, perhaps, we might even say an artistic and creative coherence. The obsessive who performs his gestures and attends to his so-called rituals is probably behaving in a perfectly coherent manner within his own system, but these movements are not part of an interaction, a dance with another. The fabric between the others and him, and him and the others, is thus torn. Moreover, if the person's entire subjectivity becomes incoherent, he undergoes a whole range of states of perplexity, confusion, irreconcilable dilemmas, blockages, splits, divisions and so on. A process of disintegration, separation, splitting and redistribution of these fragmentary elements occurs.

It is not fair to say that if you scratch the surface we are all crazy on an unconscious level. Of course, if our so-called unconscious begins to express itself in terms incompatible with our need to share it with others or, on the other hand, if others show themselves incapable of recognising the expressiveness of our subjectivity and, as far as they are concerned, we are not tuned in to the same wavelength as them and we are indeed in a world that is not the same as theirs, then yes, the question of being insane, schizophrenic, psychotic arises. But this does not mean that if we probe the depths of our minds in a more radical or more honest way we will discover that we are in fact all crazy. This means instead that, as some would say, we wear a mask. It must be remembered that we are talking about madness in the sense of what we might call social madness, not in the sense of what a Buddhist would call metaphysical madness – in the latter case, of complete social adaptation to particular formalisms "taken as embodied metaphors, without seeing them as metaphors" that according to any other group of people's categories of reality would appear as mad as any other mad behaviour.

Caretti: *You spoke of the need for a 'journey' to get back in touch with that inner reality that we lost a long time ago. In your opinion, can madness also be considered as a kind of journey into the unconscious? And what does the therapist become in this case? A guide, a sorcerer?*

Laing: I would not define madness as a journey into the unconscious. Our minds always harbour the misleading tendency to think in terms of the individual person when we talk about schizophrenia, madness or sanity and the like. We must bear in mind that language constantly leads us into the error that in *Being and Nothingness* Sartre imputes to Hegel and Heidegger, even to Husserl. That is, the error of speaking of the subjectivity of person X as if it were not intersubjective, as if it could be extrapolated from the universe as an essence, as a thing in itself.

However, I am convinced that some people experience extremely unpleasant mental states of bewilderment and/or false lucidity. Essentially, the only way for them to get out of it is to conquer the capacity to look, that is, to simply pay attention to what is happening, without doing anything. Call it Zen, Chan, Satipatthana, it does not matter. If they can somehow manage to let go, without superimposing their own whims, then out of all this chaos a little order seems to begin to emerge.

And some seem to go through a series of transformations of the kind that Jung first described in *Symbols of Transformation*, and then come out of it and overcome the chaos. John Perry, Joseph Campbell and several others have put forward the idea that if you do not interfere with the mind of a person diagnosed as schizophrenic but just stay there with it, letting whatever wants to emerge eventually emerge, a sequence comparable to the sequences described in myths and rituals all over the world occurs.

I would prefer to call this ordered set of transformations, as Jung does in *Symbols of Transformation*, a process of metanoia. One can think of the difference between a wrecked ship and a sinking ship, one which one can still try to empty of the water it takes in, which one can plug up and which one can then get moving and perhaps have towed into port. A shipwreck or a total catastrophe is no longer a journey. I mean the trouble with many of the most severely disturbed people we see in London is that they are not engaged in any journey at all; on the contrary, we are faced with bits of wreckage or endlessly rushing about alone. It is a never-ending quarrel between one side of the face and the other, or between one hand and the other. If this situation is unblocked, or if that transcendent function of the Self which Jung speaks of as the central factor in healing begins to manifest, then the mandala-like archetypal forms we have mentioned emerge and these people see their world take on an order. Unfortunately, it is often an order that is judged to be psychotic. But a re-ordering seems possible, leading back to a state in which the person co-exists with others in a socially acceptable way.

Caretti: *In* The Politics of Experience, *you said that those who have survived the journey through madness unscathed possess exceptional qualities of evaluation of the domains of spirit they inhabit. Do you consider yourself a survivor of this journey?*

Laing: I have never been psychotic. My inner adventures, which continue to this day, have never led me to a state that can be called psychotic. What counts is not so much the content, but what you do with it. Suppose a guy sees someone in this room who is not there. Well, I would not call him psychotic for that reason. But if he insists that I have seen that someone too, despite my assertion to the contrary, then I would probably start to get irritated. If he then claims that what I say to him is influenced by what this 'other' person has said to me, then I would be willing to admit the possibility that we live in a psychosphere and that I am perhaps receiving messages from some psychic source of which I am not aware, which is hypnotically inducing me to react in a certain way to the person in question. I would judge this as decidedly implausible but I would not rule it out entirely. In short, before I start calling him insane, he should manifest every possible kind of socially disjunctive behaviour.

And this judgement of madness would depend not only on what this person experiences but also on how he interprets his own experience and how he expresses himself in the construction he builds on the basis of his own experience in relation to others. Only at this point, in the face of such an impressive array of disorderly phenomena would I say that the person in question is psychotic.

Caretti: *There is a very beautiful Zen saying: "He who has lost his life will find it." Do not you think that the experience of madness can be seen as a process of death-rebirth of the individual?*

Laing: Let us leave aside the Christian tradition for the moment and talk about those other traditions that are so much in vogue today. Let us pause regarding the crucial experience of death and rebirth, death and resurrection or beginning and end. Now it must be said at once that these traditions do not suggest that in the process one should become insane.

The point is that some people actually experience extremely unpleasant states of confusion and mental opacity. While they are in them they are almost completely unable to play their part in everyday social exchanges. It is often recommended that those who enter such a phase should withdraw from the world for some time, as far as possible. I mean to cut off all relationships, isolate oneself or enter a monastery, where the person in a state of confusion will find individuals who have themselves gone through that same experience and are able to assist one who is going through it for a period of time, perhaps for years. It should be borne in mind, however, that all these expedients (for example, the choice to isolate oneself) have the sole purpose of avoiding the risk of going insane related to the attempt to maintain the usual relationships with others when our mind has entered such a different space and to the excessive pressure that may result.

The moments of death and rebirth – whether or not they are understood in the Jungian sense, which is essentially a translation of Christian theology into psychological terms – take place independently of our efforts. When it happens it happens, no matter how great the effort we put into the practice of meditation. It is not a goal towards which we can direct our steps. No matter how hard we try, and despite all the pleasure these efforts may give us, this death is not suicide but rather something to which we must submit. We try in the most subtle ways to evade this submission to a death that perhaps comes from within us but from outside our ego. The ego cannot commit suicide; if we try to commit psychological suicide, we go mad. But it is possible to adopt the attitude of someone who is prepared to accept his own death.

There is nothing so very remote or difficult about the death of the ego. As Freud and Jung pointed out, we die (in this sense) every time we fall asleep. But the ego can also dissolve outside of sleep simply by sitting up, emptying the mind and focusing attention on an object, a thing or even a theme, as when we absorb ourselves in a mantra. What is more, the ego disappears in a state of full waking consciousness. One cannot find one's ego. One may not even look for it, but if one did, one would not find it. One is dead. Or we can go beyond that, into the last zone of Visuddhi-Magga.[24] Here we find ourselves in a state in which consciousness and space are indistinguishable and consciousness can only register consciousness, but it becomes in this situation consciousness of nothing. One is dead and it is from here that one reconstitutes himself. Apart from the special gradualness which is proper to meditation this happens, it seems to me, every time we are given an anaesthetic, as for example in the dentist's chair. A dissolution takes place, although not in sleep or unconsciousness. We have lost the ego with which we identify ourselves.

Art consists in setting out on the way of this loss of the ego without going mad, either before, during or after. So one who finds himself plunged into disorientation and bewilderment or wandering around like a hungry spectre, or the person who has died and is desperately trying to be reborn, is simply one who has not gone through the whole cycle of this death and resurrection, but has been caught in some intermediate moment. Irrespective of the specific tactics, the clever devices that one can adopt in dealing with a person in such a situation, what we may call the function of the guide or therapist is in principle identical with that of the meditation master. The essential point is what one is able to give (whatever it is) to the other person through one's presence, that is, through a relationship with this simple presence (and nothing else). The problem is to get the other person to stand up and get back on track.

To say that madness is *the* 'journey' would be a terrible confusion. I have already said, but I would like to repeat, that many who are insane are people who have lost their way. Perhaps, in retrospect, this losing their way may appear as part of the way they were meant to take.

Caretti: *Alright, but then what is the way?*

Laing: There is no way of telling which is the way. But we have reports of people who have gone through singular, exceptional mental states and come back from them. There is therefore the possibility, albeit very uncertain, of establishing some generalisations about the sequences that one goes through. Then there is the *Tibetan Book of the Dead*, which tells us about some of these things. And Jung's *Mysterium Conjunctionis* (one of his last works) puts forward the idea that alchemical sequences offer important keys when read as metaphors for the transformations that take place in the human soul under certain circumstances. From all this we have perhaps gained an idea of the schema of the process. But it is a very rough idea. That is to say, we are not able to provide a map and explain to those concerned that they are at a place X and that, if they want to get to a place Y, they have to follow a certain way. We use the word 'way' but in reality we are perhaps already beyond what we can talk about. We are in the Chan, in Zen, in the Tao. The way we can talk about is not the way. The true way is in any case absolutely unique and individual.

I do not claim that madness is the same thing as an LSD trip. This is an idea that has been attributed to me and also to the work I do here in London with Leon Redler and other colleagues, but which I have always rejected. An acid trip, even one in which there is a disintegration or disruption of our usual sensory organisation (sight, hearing, taste, smell), in which our relationship with others is deranged, in which space and time dissolve, has nothing to do with being insane.

What can happen with LSD is that someone under the influence of acid loses control of his nerves and blows out, falling prey to panic or begins to grasp, to hold on to this or that fragment or shred of reality, thus passing into a frenzied state of mind. More than just losing himself, he loses his balance, becoming unable to coordinate what he says about where he is, with how others interpret his words and no longer able to understand others with respect to their language, which he misinterprets as his own. Ultimately, what he expresses is misunderstood and what others express he takes to mean something else. Once again, the mutual connective link of being together is lost here and we find ourselves in the realm of psychosis. It is a catastrophe, which resembles a journey into madness like taking a car and crashing it into a wall. It is a departure and a shipwreck or a collision in the course of the journey. Then it is a question of how the pieces are put back together with the hope that the journey will end with the arrival of a rescue team. This is a catastrophe that can happen during an LSD session, and very often the problem arises not in the middle of the journey but on the way back. If this gets stuck, one can be caught in two different mental states simultaneously: still being on the road yet being, in a sense, back to normal. A deep, tormenting sense of perplexity and anguish may persist and contribute to this situation. Again the possibility of madness arises, but this does not mean that madness is any more advisable than shipwrecking or falling off a mountain. So we cannot really say that it is a journey into madness. Madness is not the goal, nor is it an intermediate station on the way to enlightenment. A forced passage through it may perhaps, in some cases, be part of the journey. But this does not mean that the watchword 'set a course for madness' is right, because madness would represent the collapse of our false social order and through it we would tear the world apart and rebuild a better one. No, whatever the situation – the world may be shattered or wavering and we may be in a state of frenzy or panic – our attempt is always to recover our presence of mind in coping with our experience, whatever it holds out for us. Think of the Buddha, who was tormented by his horrible visions but did not sink into madness because of them. The point is not so much that undergoing visions, hallucinations and transformations of time and space (phenomena that often occur spontaneously whether in meditation, under the influence of LSD or even in ordinary life) leads to madness. The important thing is not to allow these phenomena to take over.

Thank goodness (and knock on wood!), as far as I can remember this has never happened to me. But on several occasions I have felt that I have been a hair's breadth away from losing myself completely in it all. But there is worse than that. There is a sense in which the lostness of the individual is lost in an even more diabolically confused world. As for me, I do not recommend that anyone undertake journeys into these regions of the universe.

Caretti: *It occurs to me that one of the fundamental positions of Hatha Yoga is called* Savasana *and it means 'the one who is dying'. Do you not think we should start learning 'to die' in order to open ourselves up to existence, as Jaspers suggested?*

Laing: I prefer to avoid statements like "We all have to die". I suppose there must be innumerable transformations, I mean mental transformations. Those who wish to reckon with them can turn to Visuddhi-Magga, Mahayana and post-Mahayana Buddhism, which are engaged in the scholarly study of the most subtle distinctions of different states of consciousness.

One way of illustrating this sequence of transformations is to take our ego (which, it seems to me, is what we are talking about) and suppose it to be a function of consciousness state 1 (or C_1). So in C_1 we have the ego 1 (or E_1). The ego is a function of C_1, is co-ordinated with its structure and exists only within it (i.e. is part of that mental context). An isolated ego, which can wander into other worlds, does not exist. The ego is an element of C_1. Let us now use the word 'world' instead of 'consciousness'. The world that C_1 builds will be W_1 of which our ego is an element. If we want to get out of W_1, we have to lose E_1. And if we want to lose E_1, we must necessarily lose W_1 as well. The one goes with the other. Let us now suppose that we set out to lose E_1 through meditation. E_1 then disappears and with it W_1. But E_1 is replaced by E_2 in W_2. In order to attain even the simplest of those mental states which the Teravada Buddhists would call Nirvana one has to go through a whole series of such transformations. That is, you have to go through E_1, E_2, E_3, E_4 and so on, until you reach E_0 and W_0, in which there is no longer any world, no person, no mind, no thought, no phenomenon.

Of course, we are talking about an experience that is not of concern to everyone, only those who have reached the stage of mental development that makes the state described the inevitable natural next step on the path of the individual. In my opinion, anyone who wants to be a master in psychology, in the Buddhist sense, must necessarily have experienced a wider purview than that of ordinary worldly consciousness. And yet, this ordinary consciousness is by no means to be despised (Buddhists would say it is not to be avoided). But if, while sitting, we gaze fixedly at any single element of it, we find that it dissolves. Not because we are striving to get rid of it. It simply disappears, whether we want it to or not. Eventually, in meditation one can repeat this pendular movement in which ordinary consciousness continually emerges and disappears.

Of course, pursuing these states is in itself what Trungpa recently called a different form of spiritual materialism (or spiritual technology) and a different form of greed. And there is today a whole market for these things, offering, Deleuze would say, alternate fare. Since we are all saying today that we are in a state of confusion and ignorance, that the contradictions of capitalism have overwhelmed us and so on. So the message is: "You may think you are happy, but remember earlier this morning or last night – it is all one big lie. But be aware that trying to cure yourself is very dangerous." The *game* is then to sell you 'experts', people who have studied these things for a long, long time and have graduated from a Zen monastery or something like that. And another group of professional experts will take care to convince your mind to take this journey on its own so that, duly helped, you can wait for death. So we are in the business not only of our physical death but of our spiritual and egoic death. In a sense, a new system of indulgences has taken shape. People are oppressed because they are made to feel that they are inadequate or that in their ordinary state of consciousness they surely do damage and, in such a confusion, how could they not spread misery and destruction all around them? Especially if they do not realise it, for sin (it is believed) is that thing of which the less you know you are in, the more you are in it. So a new Nietzschean priest figure emerges, intimidating everyone with this doctrine, overpowering even the most powerful warlord, forcing him to kiss his feet and beg "Please, help me." It is very easy to fall into it, with the risk of creating a new kind of thanatologist. It is enough to look at the death industry, transformed almost into a tourist industry. I do not like this side of the phenomenon at all.

Caretti: *How do you view the therapeutic use of LSD and Stanislav Grof's work in this field in the United States?*

Laing: I think this is extremely important. I do not know of anything comparable. It is a pity that research of such a high level has been discontinued. I know Grof, we have met several times, although the most recent things we have talked about at any length are what he discusses in the first volume of *Realms of the Human Unconscious*,[25] which I find to be flawless. I mean flawless in the sense that the bulk of the book consists of an honest report of the experiences of a variety of people. And this brings me back to the question of scientific freedom.

Psychology must have its own space. In other words, in any discussion of LSD it must be said that people experience themselves phenomenologically as returning to childhood, birth or even our intrauterine stages. Under the influence of acid we relive our foetal and embryonic stages, experience our conception and even experience ourselves, prior to this, as spermatozoa or eggs. A mysterious leap then occurs which leads to experiencing oneself before incarnation (i.e. in states of bardic consciousness), to experiencing deaths related to previous lives or the events of those lives. What is more, it is even possible to recall experiences completely outside the human sphere, to experience oneself as any moment of the phylogenetic tree: as a vegetable, as a mineral, as pure energy. Finally, one comes to experience oneself as potentially no longer present in our physical world, be it a phenomenal world or a world of energy fields. John Lilly reported his own direct experiences of this kind in *The Center of the Cyclone*[26] and elsewhere. In the early psychedelic literature we find all these things.

But Grof's sober, balanced and accurate report of this area of human experience has opened up (if we do not want to say widened or exalted) the reality of these transformations. They come again and again, and they are not random. Although it is very difficult to predict what will happen to a given individual, I believe that Grof has typologically organised at least 99.9 percent of the experiences people have had with acid under the specific conditions he has created. Grof does not even examine the psychosocial range of experiences that other people have had with acid in completely different conditions. But, within their limits his observations are very important, even from the relatively narrow perspective of psychopharmacology. There is no doubt that, despite all the restrictions, psychopharmacological research will see great developments in the next decade, thanks in part to a Latin American psychiatrist[27] who has considerably deepened his knowledge of the different chemical composition of the drugs used by sorcerers in Latin American countries: LSD, mescaline, psilocybin, yage and others. He then tried to correlate the various experiential transformations induced by these drugs with the different characteristics of the triggering chemical agent. Another result of Grof's research, it seems to me, is to show that the idea of employing LSD in psychotherapy is scientifically respectable, and perfectly acceptable. But a great deal of work was done in this field in the 1950s and 1960s, and it seems to me to be very promising.

I think that Grof's theories of a co-existence and of perinatal matrices are both very useful formulations, although as far as I am concerned, I am not convinced that they have been elaborated in a complete or definitive way. I am not sure, for example, that what he considers as part of the perinatal matrix is not a condensation of more things than just birth. It is not difficult to imagine a development of Grof's formula into peri-death matrices of various kinds. Nor is it too difficult to think of a peri-conception, peri-implantation matrix, or a matrix around the early development of the cardiovascular system. This thing – the first time the pulsating stream emerges within us, differentiated from the rest of us– seems to be of great importance. Indeed, all the major embryological stages, and particularly conception, lend themselves to this kind of theorising.

In this country there is a very interesting man called Frank Lake, who in the 1950s wrote a book called *Clinical Theology*.[28] In this book, Lake deals with the experience of death and rebirth in relation to the corresponding Christian doctrine. During the 1950s and early 1960s he used a great deal of LSD; in fact, more than anyone else I know, more as far as I know than even Tim Leary or Grof, and far more than I. Now Lake works on birth rituals and takes people to primary birth experiences. He is open to anything such people might find themselves involved in once they let go. He is also convinced that whatever people have reported under the influence of acid can also happen without it and within the context of his practice. I think it greatly expands the meaning of what Grof has already observed. Lake has highlighted the breadth of the contemporary Western mind that becomes accessible during the acid sessions administered by him, but I think it is safe to assume that this has relevance outside of a connection with acid as well. Far from being merely a study of acid, the research has much wider implications. One of these implications is this, that a person, in order to get rid of the tormenting situation in which he finds himself in W_1, can dissolve W_1 and realise that it is not the only state in which he can find himself, that therefore it is a mental product.

The real problem, therefore, is above all that of integrating this awareness into one's subsequent life; that is, after one's return, no matter whether from an acid experience; from a rebirth ritual; from a journey into the spaces into which the various forms of so-called primary or radical therapy take us; or, again, from a meditative or perhaps spontaneous experience. Again, Grof is perfectly aware of this. I think this kind of work is bearing very important, and very salutary, fruit.

DIALOGUE 8
Language, Time, Silence

Caretti: *You said that language is essentially made up of knots, of tangles of words, Maya's machinations that mask the true meaning of things. Language therefore seems to generate illusions. On the other hand, Sartre quotes Heidegger, saying with him: "I am what I say."*

Laing: I confess that I am not sure what can be called language, nor of what we have at our disposal. I am not sure I can really define what language is, nor understand when different people use the word 'language'. They do not seem to mean the same thing, and the disagreement about how to conceive of the nature of language is considerable. Is music a language? Let us ask the question: Is there a language of music or can there be a musical language? There are numerous musical conventions that possess a coherent set of transformations and rules, and it is probably legitimate to speak of a grammar and syntax of music. Let us ask again: Is there a language of gesture? Is there a language of dance? The anthropologist Roy Birdwhistell[29] argues for the existence of a syntactic system of gesture and general bodily movement, the subject of a branch of anthropology to which he gives the name of 'kinesics'. There are therefore kinesic languages and sonic languages; but what is the relationship between this visual-auditory system and what it means? I am not sure that I understand the different notions of the sign, nor what the relationship between signified and signifier is, nor what different aspects are to be recognised in any elementary operation of a binary language: numerical operations, analogical operations, etc. Some say that dreams are a language. In his book on dreams,[30] Erich Fromm adopted the expression 'forgotten language', implying that there are other kinds of elements besides phonemes and notes, or the intervals between notes or the intervals between tones. We have already said that there are those who speak without embarrassment of the 'language' of a dream. Systems of all kinds are thus qualified as languages, and if we retain the single term of 'language', it must be said that there are languages of different kinds and not only spoken languages, to which the current use of the word refers. So if music is to be considered as a language, it is a peculiar kind of language. In fact, compared to a discursive utterance, it probably has a different relationship with sonic matter, that is, sonic matter has a different relationship with what is communicated.

Like certain linguistic theories, it is difficult to say where the distinction can be made between an emotional utterance – which may, logically speaking, be entirely tautological and have no truth value of any kind – and a melody, or the like. In short, my thinking about language remains incoherent, fragmentary.

The depiction of language as a net goes back to Plotinus. I can no longer tell whether he is talking about the words themselves or the ideas or forms assumed by our minds. Or perhaps the sense is that our mind casts a net into the ocean but does not capture it. In this case, the image alludes to the frequently described error of confusing the grid of a map with what the grid covers, the border marks with the territory, the menu with the meal.

In spite of all the epistemological errors of which the very existence of language opens up the possibility, there would be no epistemology without language, and I do not think it is permissible to go so far as to say that language is in itself some kind of gigantic epistemological error. If we stop for a moment to think in biological terms, we realise that it has an evolutionary significance. We must reflect, it seems to me, on the survival value of language, and the survival function that language performs for us is certainly not only that of transmitting the truth. Indeed, according to the suggestion of some linguists, language may have originated as a means of deception and enticement, for example, for purposes of imitation or mimesis in the game between hunter and prey, between man and man. It would be pure naivety to think that the ordinary function of language has specifically to do with truth. And if this is sometimes the case, it is not necessarily always the case. The confusion of the shadow with that which casts the shadow is repeated here. There is no reason to abolish the shadow, nor, so to speak, to censor it, nor even to become incapable of being fascinated or moved by a dance of shadows.

Language is something I cannot imagine being without. It is something I am deeply grateful for. I prefer being able to speak to being mute, just as I prefer having the ability to think to not having it. Of course, I am then glad if I can rest from thinking now and then, but that is no reason not to appreciate the joy of it. Thinking leads us to all the errors whose possibility is implicit in thinking itself, and these errors are undoubtedly legion. David Hume, reflecting on thinking, states that every thought added to another according to any nexus or chain or line of thoughts increases the probability of error, and warns against it. This is the sceptical position of thought with regard to itself; that is, the position of thought that questions its own validity, with the consequence that it must then question the validity of this questioning of its own validity, and so on. This way, too, does not seem to me to lead far. Nor does the fact that one often enjoys silence suffice to decide that speech is a bad thing. Certainly, talking all the time becomes unbearable in the long run, and there are those who never seem to tire of dialogue or even of monologising. Some people get into a frenzy. These things undoubtedly happen. Nevertheless, I am grateful for language. I cannot get out of language, but I do not hate it for that, because to get out of it is to find oneself reduced to nothing, to emptiness. I am not sure I fully understand the saying "I am what I say" but I think language is intrinsic to all thought, that it is the form taken by thinking. I cannot conceive of any thought I may have that is not in some sense, let us say, part of me, and is not on the other hand intrinsically an expression of a coherent system of meaning-bearing relationships. I am therefore reconciled with language. I am grateful for it and I think I appreciate it more than I used to. Language is, in Heidegger's words, the house in which, as human beings, we live. We dwell in language; it is the habitat of our mind. The world comes to us through the scrim or filter of language. It is language that allows us to express and communicate our love as well as our hatred or resentment.

Caretti: *The way of silence has always been the way of the great masters. In fact, the Tao Te Ching opens with this sentence: "The Tao that can be told is not the eternal Tao." Wittgenstein said in the* Tractatus *that "what can be shown, cannot be said".[31] Even you have said that the meaning of true experience is silence. What is silence for you?*

Laing: Take music, sound and silence. In his *Notebook for Anna Magdalena Bach*, Bach wrote pieces of music that any young boy beginning to learn the piano can easily play. In two or three pages he explains the core of his musical theory, highlighting how in his music (which is contrapuntal music) the elements that constitute its form and meaning are not the notes but the relationships between the notes. It is the ratio of an octave followed by the ratio of a sixth, followed by the ratio of a third, followed by the ratio of a fifth…

Listening to Bach, or any other music, you start by hearing the notes. But if you transpose a melody, whistling or humming it (which more or less we all know how to do), to a different key, it becomes evident, even if you may not be fully aware of it, that what you are reacting to and translating in your own way, is the relationship between the notes and not the notes themselves. Now the relationship between notes is not a note. Indeed, this relation is not a sound but the relation between two sounds. And what is the opposite of sound? Obviously silence. The fact is, then, that notes create a shimmering illusion, shaping silence into different textures or modules. What counts in the end is the interval between the notes, that is, the silence. It makes no noise but it is what we hear, what we grasp as an octave or as a perfect fifth.

And what we perceive or register is a difference, and precisely a difference in our input. So information is news of a difference. There is a difference and then there is another difference, which is another interval. We can thus record the news of the difference between two differences and so on. That is, we catch not only the difference A-B or C-D but the difference between these differences, thus obtaining the difference E-F. And there is then a difference between the difference C-D and the difference E-F, as well as between A-B and E-F. Let us then take the difference between the differences A-B and C-D, and the difference between the differences C-D and E-F, and compare these differences. How far our mind can go on this path I cannot say. I must say that my imagination stops here and sometimes I can only follow my memory.

The same, it seems to me, happens with space, that is, with line, contour. So the difference between two colours is not a colour, not indeed something we see with our eyes, but only a comparison between different things we see. To conclude, and returning to the example of music, we can in a certain sense say that music has an anamnestic function of the Platonic type, that of reminding us, by playing with our ears, that what the fabric of sound reveals is the ocean of silence. And this ocean – that is, simply a weft of silence – is also the precondition of language.

Caretti: *In everything you say there is always a tragic component. Your work seems to be shot through with the anxiety of time. Do you think we can free ourselves from this terror?*

Laing: Before answering it is necessary to stop for a moment. First of all, I would like to know for sure whether you use the word 'anxiety' as an English equivalent of the Heideggerian *Sorge*. In fact the currently differently used terms – and in particular *Angst* and *Sorge* – are understood by different people in different ways.

Personally, I have happily reconciled with time, although I hesitate to say so out loud. In short, today I am quite at ease with time. It is more of a friend than an enemy and it offers me a benign face. Like language, time is in a sense what we find ourselves in. It all depends on whether we take it as a welcome environment, as a home, or whether we feel exiled in it, imprisoned. As for me, I do not feel it to be a Siberia of the mind. Of course, however eternity may be conceived, I do not think it can be said that it is time that lasts forever. I mean our temporality is disfigured by our mortality and therefore time is not merely a theoretical problem. We do not have all the time in the world. We all have to die and this is necessarily a source of existential *pathos*. It is not just a question of death but of the passing of all things, of growing old and, in the end, only of dying. At one time it seemed to me – and indeed, I suppose, it still seems to me, only it no longer depresses me as much as it did in the past – that the mark of time was generally, and perhaps always and in every respect, a mark of vanity which brands everything as transient, as *vanitas vanitatum*. The comparison of what you feel matters as an absolute must with the dissolution of all things seems to be a painful thought. And it is certainly a thought with which the human mind has sometimes refused to reconcile itself, keeping only one of the two terms and suppressing the other.

On the other hand, the very pleasure of living undoubtedly contains an element of adventure, tension and risk. So that without the possibility of dying now, at this moment, and without the inevitability of death sooner or later, I cannot imagine any enjoyment. In other words, the experience of breathlessness and anxiety over time is certainly full of pain and regret. But that nothing lasts forever is also the precondition of our being happy.

Being a human being does not grieve me, nor does having to die. I do not think I have any reason to fear the fact of death, only perhaps its possible manner. A mathematician once told me that he thought it was not difficult to reconcile oneself with the fact that we are mortal. But how can one be reconciled as easily with the thought that one day the universe will cease to exist, and there will be no trace of the *homo sapiens*? Personally, I can be reconciled with this thought. If I may put it this way: I have no difficulty in imagining that the rest of the universe will not be at all embarrassed to reconcile itself to the disappearance of the human race. I really do not see that it has contributed much to the growth and survival of the world as a whole.

Caretti: *Jung liked to say that when a man knows more than others, he withdraws into his interior silence. You, too, after searching all these years for a scientific hypothesis that would make the facts of human experience intelligible, wrote that "We come back to ourselves as our own final* *authority".*[32] *Does this going back mean for you a necessary introversion or is it instead a new revelation about existence?*

Laing: These terms 'internal' and 'external' and all the others that are connected with them, such as 'introversion' and 'extroversion', are clearly figures of speech. But in reality it is not at all about penetrating into our body, or at any rate into the space we are talking about. It is not easy to disentangle mental space from space (whatever that may be) as we experience it.

If I penetrate into my mind, this does not necessarily mean that I penetrate into my cranium. Nor does looking directly into me mean looking at how I see. But in "how I see what I see" I probably look at what I see. In other words, if I am examining my phenomenal world – and therefore in a sense I am looking outside – then the room is not in my head or in my consciousness. The room is out there and no other experiential room is given, in any sense. As for the double of this room of which Eddington speaks, made up of atoms and molecules, it may be an imaginary room, but this imaginary room is no more in my head than the phenomenal room is. It, too, is out there, in front of me. As I said before, the sense of the original foundation or deep and abyssal ground of our personal being is necessarily related to the foundation – or deep ground or origin or source – of everything else. To say I am not part of all this, therefore, seems to me an incomprehensible statement. I simply cannot see how one can think one is not, when it is so obvious that one is. Of course, the individual is separated from his own personal peculiarities, his own physicality, which he experiences in his own particular way, but at the same time every single molecule in his body is in vibration with cosmic fields of various kinds, which physicists are increasingly identifying. In other words, saying we are part of the tapestry is still not enough. It is too static a representation of this interpenetration of forces. Our bodies are completely porous and extremely reactive to electric or magnetic fields and so on. These are things on which a great deal of research has been done in recent times.

I do not look at myself as 'more internal' or 'more external'. It makes no sense for me to say that I withdraw into myself or find myself. Indeed, I am the one I am looking for, but I am also the one who is looking. It is a bit like asking a hand to grasp itself. If I have lost myself, who is the 'I' who has lost himself? Who is this 'I' who should be the subject of the research? No spatial image is entirely appropriate to this situation, not that of the dog trying to bite its own tail; not that of the Ouroboros, that is, the serpent with its tail in its mouth; nor that of a circular movement. All these figures, and the geometrical representations and images of circular movement provide us with nothing more than an allusion. They are incapable of expressing the thing. And whoever has attempted to do so has always made it clear that what he says is to be taken with a certain amount of humour, and not literally. But worse things happen. It happens (and in modern philosophy it is certainly a frequent occurrence) that those who are engaged in such an attempt are unable to say anything that makes sense. Indeed, Ayer or Quine would say that all assertions of this kind are the very paradigm of what is totally meaningless.

DIALOGUE 9
On the Part of Young People and Women

Caretti: *The revolt of the young radicals in the 1960s was an attempt to fill the gap between objective social awareness and subjective inner reality through new cultural models. In what sense were you part of that revolt and what contributions do you think you made to the ideologies of the new generations?*

Laing: Of all the things you have asked me so far, the one that lends itself best to a clear-cut answer is this one. The mere fact of your question and this interview is evidence of my contribution to that ideology. As for my contributions in terms of activism, or the movements that characterise the 1960s in particular, three seem to me to be most clearly identifiable. The first concerns the protests, especially the student protests in America against the atomic bomb, against Washington's Cuban policy and against the war in Vietnam and Cambodia. The second concerns the movement related to drugs and acid, and the third student activism in Europe, in 1968, and what followed, up to that form of extreme politicisation of student movements which in various countries went as far as adopting a strategy of urban guerrilla warfare or terrorism. I had relations with some of the people in all these movements, but I did not take an active part in any of them. My attitude has been different in the various cases and never entirely congenial. I will try to briefly summarise my relationship with some of these phenomena.

First of all there are my links with the new English Left, which used especially my exposition of Sartre's thought – and as far as I was concerned was perfectly entitled to do so, given the compatibility between my ideas and theirs. But I also knew several of them personally and was able to provide detailed analyses of micropolitical situations, with their interactions and dialectics, which they appreciated. In empirically oriented Marxism one has to look at things in detail as well as globally, and also at small-scale political structures, albeit placing them in their broader context. So my kind of work interested them. On the other hand, I had nothing to do, in a direct way, with the peace movements, with activities aimed at ending the war in Asia, limiting armaments and the like. I have never taken an active part in all this, in any way, as Chomsky or Sartre, for example, have done. Of course, I have always felt solidarity with these movements, but I have never sympathised very much with their way of acting. It has always been absolutely clear to me that marching down Fifth Avenue to Central Park and holding a demonstration could only provoke the police to intervene, with the result that they would be in a stronger position than ever to demand the deployment of the most up-to-date and sophisticated technology for the surveillance and control of the population. What is more, such movements could only generate countermovements that would aggravate, or so it seemed to me, the state of affairs against which the protest was being raised. Moreover, there were those who said that this was precisely what was wanted: to accelerate the confrontation, to precipitate a clash.

Now, although there are a number of things I do not like about capitalism (I am neither oblivious nor cynical about its brutalities and horrors), I have to say that in the relative peace and quiet of London we can sit down to talk about capitalism better than would be possible anywhere else. I know I would not last a day in China today, nor for long in Russia. The only social system that leaves room for the kind of conversation I am fond of, that allows us to talk about how things really are, is the one we have in the West. Some will say that to refuse to condemn capitalism purely and simply is a sign of horrible self-indulgence. They will say that those who behave this way do so because capitalism allows them a comfortable and pleasant life. And they will object: what about the workers?

At no time was the prospect of war, civil war or revolution a prospect that gladdened my heart. Nor did I ever think it would make things better. Instead, I was always convinced that it could only make things worse, and much worse. I have never tried to persuade anyone to follow this path. I do not wish to provide (nor do I think I have provided) any endorsement of terrorism, guerrilla warfare or the like. For me 'revolution' means the idea, impossible and absurd, of a Surrealist revolution. What I would like would be a general change in people's attitudes and a gradual, albeit very slow, evolution of things towards a situation where everyone behaves towards each other a little better. But I have never embraced any political programme. I have never come across a ready-made one that persuaded me, and I have never been able to invent one that gave me the feeling that I could do something good in that direction. What I was saying in the 1960s was that if people really wanted to change the system, the right way was neither to drop bombs, nor to leave the social order, nor to oppose bayonets with flowers. Instead, one has to accept the system, join with the police, go to universities and study well, enter the world of business, the lawyers, the judiciary. If your intentions are really serious, and if there are enough of you, then within ten or fifteen years you get to the top positions. Once we are in positions of command, we need to study how our social, technological and economic apparatus can really function in the service of man, not to torment him. Indeed, at the time many people chose this path. Speaking of the acid period, a former CIA agent calculated that over half the men in the Carter administration had taken LSD. Well, this is a fact that may appear reassuring or alarming, depending on your point of view.

Regarding acid, the first time I took it was in 1961, with a friend (a fellow psychiatrist) who had already been through it and thought I would be interested to see what it was all about. Of course, acid had already been used extensively in medical practice before then and we had plenty of reports on it. As is always the case with new things, it was also clear that it would take some time to process and classify everything and to establish exactly what the effects and potential of acid were.

Then Tim Leary and his circle of friends and entourage came along and effectively ruined the experience. Having taken acid themselves, they gave it to prisoners, sick people in hospitals, dying people and, finally, convinced themselves that absolutely everyone should try acid. At that time it was not illegal. But they manufactured it and distributed it on a large scale, so it became illegal (the penalty for illegality was, if I am not mistaken, not the possession of the acid but precisely its manufacture without authorisation). It is still a very dark chapter in the history of the 1960s. By the way, some have said that much of the huge quantities of the stuff imported into America were paid for with CIA money.

In any case, Leary and his friends began to convince themselves that America's consciousness especially was in a shambles, so completely clouded and hardened in its own particular vectors and parameters, that it would drag the whole world into a catastrophic clash from which nuclear weapons would not be excluded. And that would be the end. This was looking increasingly likely. It is difficult to imagine today how imminent it seemed to so many people at the time, including myself. I lived as if every day could bring catastrophe. We seemed close to the last minute, to the decision to press that button that would trigger the apocalypse. So Leary and his team became convinced that the best thing to do was simply to administer acid, one way or another, in the United States, and indeed throughout the world.

To see what would happen if such a thing was attempted, an experiment was done in Berkeley and in the Bay Area around San Francisco. The story is well known. Within forty-eight hours they distributed something like three hundred thousand doses of 305mg each, mostly to young people in their twenties. The repercussions were felt for months and Height Ashbury was born out of this experience. There was a kind of crusade of teenage 'dropouts', who by any means, on foot or hitchhiking, without any signal being given came to San Francisco and did drugs, as heavily and as long as possible. That did not sound terribly convincing to me. Later one of the leaders of the movement came to me in London to propose repeating the experiment here, on a perhaps even larger scale. They regarded London (he explained) as my territory and if I said no, nothing would be done about it. I said no and nothing was done about it. If they had actually taken action in London, the consequences would probably have been considerable. Their attitude was basically expressed in the following expression: "You cannot make an omelette without breaking eggs." The reasoning was that if a few dozen people went mad or killed themselves or each other, it was an extreme case and not a normal effect of acid. So there would probably have been a few accidents, but this was minimal compared to the worldwide cataclysm that would fatally occur if that path was not followed. "Maybe you have a better idea," they said to me. I did not, but I rejected theirs anyway.

So I have never been an advocate of the acid revolution, much less of guerrilla tactics and terrorism. A couple of years ago I was in Paris at a meeting of French intellectuals and anti-psychiatrists, and during the course of the meeting I was asked to sign a petition – which had already received numerous endorsements from the participants – asking the French government to release a notorious hijacker (the fact was generally admitted). I was astonished that they put such a document under my nose for me to sign and they were shocked that I did not want to sign it. Now, I do not want to be hijacked, I do not want my family or my friends to be on a plane that is hijacked. I hope that the French government and all our governments will be able to neutralise these people so that I never have to hear about them again. In the same way, I think it is a great thing if, when I walk into the lobby of a Hilton to meet a friend, I do not have to be afraid that I am going to get slammed against the wall. I do not like these things, I do not have the stomach for them and I have never found any justification for them. I wish I could say I had nothing to do with it. I do not want to have any part in it. I do not want to be a victim of it, nor do I want to be among those who do such things. All I want is to stay away from it. I was much more sympathetic to the student movement that I had to deal with in this country in the late 1960s, because they were people who acted, for example, by organising a series of sit-ins, in an attempt to change things through an institutionalised micro-revolution, hierarchically ordered, and aimed at transforming the established institutional structure. I am convinced that these were very healthy initiatives.

If it is true, as it is, that we live, for better or for worse, in a social system that requires a centralised and bureaucratic apparatus, then what is needed is to find a way to make this apparatus truly sensitive and permeable to the needs of those it has to serve. If, in a given social group, there are certain organisational functions related to safeguarding co-ordination, consistency and order (including dealing with those who go off the rails), then a sub-set of people drawn from the total population will have to take charge of these functions.

The essential point is that this sub-group, which on the one hand administers the law and on the other hand, to a certain extent, generates it, is not above the law. The law must remain in the hands of the people (if it ever was). I think, however, that the old hereditary and individual differentiations of wealth and power are definitely changing.

The way in which the redistribution of power is implemented as the transformations underway develop does not belong to my specific field of study. And I do not want to try to sum up my ignorance in a pseudo-ideological formula. I have to accept the fact that vast social fields, with all their depth, and indeed the very social system in which I live, remain completely opaque to me. In some cases this opacity is bound to remain, because there are official secrets and therefore they are impervious to any investigation from the outside. In other words, whatever you really expect to know, you cannot know now.

Caretti: *In addition to young people, a large part of the feminist movement has also been inspired by your work. Do you think that the women's movement has contributed to solving or changing the current malaise of our civilisation?*

Laing: It may go without saying, but we have to distinguish feminists – the so-called or self-styled feminist movement – from women and women's consciousness in general. It is clear that not all women sympathise with the feminist movement or what they think the movement is. Even within the feminist movement, the differences on certain issues – for example, abortion – are considerable. There are feminists who are very strongly in favour of abortion and there are Catholic feminists, but also others, for whom abortion is ethically unacceptable.

Considering our society as I know it, if I could choose to be reincarnated as male or female, I would certainly choose to be male. Not for any reason related to the female sex but only because I believe that women, precisely because they are women, are in a more difficult situation. In a hypothetical women's society – such societies are not difficult to imagine and in fact have been theorised and propagated – in which women are the more powerful, or dominant, sex, or in which female consciousness and sensitivity set the tone for everything, my choice would probably be different.

In our society, given the difference in roles and social position of the two sexes, I think men have it easier. However, this is not to say that men do not suffer as much as women because the sexes are not entirely divided and separated. Of course, women's feelings about what is done to them reverberate in what they do to men. There is a type of male chauvinism that can be expressed and summarised in the following way: "Let us enjoy it while it lasts." Well, in my opinion, those who think in this way lose a lot. On the other hand, it is clear that as long as women are treated unfairly (largely by men), and as long as men feel that this state of affairs benefits them, it would be asking too much of human nature to expect men as a whole to look closely at the problem. As always, the only ones who can do this with the necessary tenacity are the victims of the situation. In order to begin to change things, I think, therefore, that we will need the impetus of women. As this condition continues, we can certainly expect that among them those will emerge who will take on the task of putting an end to this particular form of injustice.

I believe that this observation is in line with the principles of fair play, although I know that it is considered an expression of an old disdainful liberal bourgeois moralism. I am convinced that part of the difficulty lies in the fact that this imbalance of power between men and women, on the one hand, seems to be a function of the global context in which we live, and on the other seems to reinforce the *status quo*. The existing state of affairs can be described by pointing out that we all live in houses and cities that all have, without exception, been designed by men and built by men with materials extracted, transported and put together by males. Airplanes, automobiles, ships, the machinery and technological artefacts of all kinds that constitute the outward manifestations of our civilisation, or culture… practically all of these have been designed and built by men. We are well aware of the objections to speaking in terms of femininity or of the eternal feminine, or to attributing different attitudes and positions to women as such. Yet we all tend to forget this and to underestimate the weight of social conditioning in this area.

With regard to the control or monopoly of the marketplace by male individuals, and all its consequences, a problem seems to emerge. Women do not, on the whole, seem terribly anxious to enter this system. For example, we do not see queues of women waiting at the gates of shipyards, although they are certainly exploited as cheap labour in factories, and although in general what we may call the slave labour force of the world comprises a high percentage of women. Not to mention those occupations that are not usually considered work (in the sense that no salary is derived from them), such as housework, shopping and cooking, childcare and the like. It is a heavily unbalanced situation and certainly does not benefit women, children or men. But how to go about changing it is another matter.

Let us consider the voice of women in the field of psychology. I think it is true that psychology – let us say Freudian psychology – suffers from a very, very serious distortion. It distorts the picture and the distortion creeps into all aspects of Freud's theory. So until a balanced psychology has been worked out, the whole thing remains very suspicious. What I mean is that the theory of repression itself operates to some extent because of this distortion as a repressive theory. This is a subtle mistake, a source of serious confusion into which many fall. Again, we can only say that things have to change, and I believe that the impetus is coming from women. So far, we have had no female thinker of the calibre of Freud or Nietzsche or Schopenhauer, except perhaps Simone de Beauvoir (I am not thinking, mind you, of intellectual stature but of psychological talent). The trouble is that Freud, being, as I believe, a genius, when he makes a mistake, his mistake is a profound one. And to correct a profound mistake one must be as profound as the mistake. Which is not easy. An obvious example of such a mistake is the doctrine of penis envy in women (with which it would of course be easy to contrast womb envy in men).

I find it difficult to understand some aspects of the institutionalised practice of 'technological childbirth' without assuming that some kind of envy plays a part. It seems to me that there is an unwitting destruction of a good thing, an effort to make things more difficult rather than easier, to the point of destroying the whole birthing experience. The woman is taken away from her family, her children, her husband and put in a strange place. Then they undress her and subject her to the degrading ritual of pubic shaving, which makes her ugly. Finally – and this is the so-called final touch – they put her on her back, with her legs up and her knees in special stirrups; that is, they force her into a position that is clearly the exact opposite of the most appropriate for a woman to be in when she has to deliver her child between her legs. Talking to a group of medical students the other day, I pointed out that this position, despite the fact that it has no medical rationale whatsoever, is imposed on ninety-five percent of women throughout the world. Why? If you want to examine a woman, you can politely ask her to lie on her back with her legs up. A couple of minutes will be enough. There is no need to immobilise her, as they do in America, by restraining her wrists as well. How do you think you would feel about such treatment?

So we have a situation totally under male control, where men do to women the things we have just said, very often encouraged by the nurses. But I think women are increasingly inclined to object, and resentment of this kind of treatment is becoming more and more articulate. This is true, however, in America, for postnatal care. It is still very common for the mother and child to be separated, whether they want to be or not, and whether the father wants to be or not. Again, it is a political issue. Who owns the child at that moment? The hospital or the mother? Well, today there are doctors and nurses (although admittedly still a minority) who are convinced that it belongs to the mother. The jungle of the problem is very dense. The whole field has to be investigated inch by inch, and each problem dealt with separately. Wherever this imbalance of power and control operates, we come across sexual discrimination.

If I insist so much on this aspect, it is because in all that concerns expressiveness and articulation, awareness and consciousness, the mind certainly cannot be helped by terrorising it. Power is simply the exercise of terror; the more subtle the power, the more concealed the terror. In the people I see as most frightened, the most striking feature is that what frightens them is not open space or closed space, the sky falling on them or the earth opening up under their feet, or birds or bees or whatever. Primarily, what these people are afraid of is other people (themselves or others). Human beings are afraid of human beings. When your freedom is compromised – in the sense of the freedom to reveal, to manifest yourself, as is the case in a system where such manifestations are subject to strict limitations and controls – your mind is damaged. Far from empowering it, terror dulls the mind. If you are terrified you cannot think about anything else with calm, breadth, coherence and clarity. I believe that the crucial question in feminism is precisely that of power relations and their change.

The balance is beginning to tip a little in favour of women and I hope that this trend will continue, until a point of equilibrium is reached. If I lived in a world where all the surgeons, all the statesmen, were women, and I found myself a mere man with no control over all these things and indeed largely at their mercy, I would feel extremely uncomfortable. In America today, male hands remove over a hundred thousand uteruses a year. To realise how serious the situation is, one only has to turn the tables and think of how we would feel if female hands were removing men's genitals. In a way, what surprises me is that women put up with so much, even though I know that such an observation is very incorrect.

Caretti: *In fact, they are so scared that they literally lose their minds...*

Laing: It is true, it is undoubtedly true. To give an example, at a recent conference on lobotomy, this statistic emerged: there are three women lobotomised for every man. This cannot be explained by the assumption that women are three times more likely to lose their minds than men. And the lobotomy is only the end point. The previous stages are tranquillisers, hospitalisation and electroshock. Here we are really in a situation of zero power. You have lost everything, you are reduced to what others want to do with you, and you have no way of stopping them from doing what they like best. So if we consider undergoing a lobotomy as a real indicator of zero power, then the ratio between women and men is three to one. That is why I say I am happy to be a man in our society. I hope women will not hold it against me if I say that. In fact, with these words I express my agreement with them in a more eloquent way than any other I can conceive.

Caretti: *You described the feminine aspect of things in* The Bird of Paradise.[33] *Can you finally clarify who this mythical bird is for you?*

Laing: I do not remember ever giving a definition of the feminine side of things. I do not know where you got that idea.

Caretti: *The Italian translator of* The Bird of Paradise *pointed out in a note that the word 'bird' has a feminine connotation, adding that in the text 'bird' always alludes to the feminine aspect of things.*

Laing: Ah, I understand. But my Italian translator got it wrong. Of course, English does not have genders and 'bird' is neither masculine nor feminine, or it can be both, but it is probably more often thought of as feminine. In colloquial language, 'bird' designates a young and attractive woman. In Italian, it seems to me, the corresponding word is masculine. So I guess what the Italian translator was trying to explain is that if you read the English word, the main resonance is perhaps feminine. But it is not a particularly strong colouring. It is true that once or twice in the text there is an exchange of lines between a person and a bird, where the bird is a girl passing by. It would be very difficult to render in Italian the association that immediately arises in an Englishman between 'bird of paradise' and 'bird' as a woman. I cannot imagine how it could be done. Yet, for me, in writing that text there was no conscious desire to identify the bird of paradise with, say, a feminine principle, however understood.

The whole matter is, to say the least, much more concrete. It came to me from a dream, in which a bird flashed before my eyes, which in the dream I took to be a bird of paradise. In fact, in the dream the only evidence of the bird's presence was a feather, which I discerned with great vividness. To retain the memory of it, I drew it. If I am not mistaken, in literature the bird of paradise often appears without legs. It cannot perch but only fly. Again, this does not necessarily hint at a particular allusion. I suppose that since this world is not exactly a Paradise or a Garden of Eden (in fact this world is usually called 'Earth' as opposed to Hell and Heaven, although we sometimes think that all these characterisations are part of our existence), there is a sense of nostalgia for a possible illusory memory of a paradisiacal condition. A bird, or a woman, or the human soul as a butterfly, can be a symbol of this. In a love relationship we may sometimes feel that the other is a nuncio of paradise, and that nostalgia may be born within us. Purely sexual passion can sometimes awaken in us the trace or perhaps almost the taste (or, put another way, the hallucinatory fantasy) of a memory of paradise. I suppose, therefore, that for a female reader the bird may well be more male than female, while for a man it is probably more female than male.

Caretti: *As an epigraph to* The Bird of Paradise *you have included a passage from the Gospel according to Thomas, in which Jesus seems to presage the birth of the 'new man' with the advent of the androgynous. Do you think, like the Jungian Erich Neumann, that the creative man is the one who has recovered and integrated his feminine aspect?*

Laing: This is perfectly true if we think of the Taoist diagram which represents the play of light and shadow, and in which there are two epicentres, the dark and the white, both rotating around the centre of circulation of energy. It seems to me that Freud and Jung are right when they say that psychologically we are all hermaphrodites, that the soul is both male and female in both men and women. It is difficult to say what masculine and feminine are, since every possible concrete example bears such deep social imprints. But if it is still permissible to speak of a masculine and a feminine principle (without defining their content), then we must recognise that they are balanced in the nature of both men and women. When a man and a woman meet, there is an intimate intertwining of the feminine side of him and the masculine side of her, as well as the feminine side of him and her, and so on with all possible combinations. Thus the masculine and feminine sides of both interact, in both a homo- and heterosexual sense. The relationship of man and woman thereby brings about completeness.

I do not know if it is really possible – I think it is very difficult anyway – to avoid absorbing some kind of deformation from our social conditioning. There are extreme cases. For example, there is a type of man who likes women a lot, and yet we can almost define him as a male lesbian. Sometimes he may give the impression of being a homosexual man, but in fact he has no interest in men. He is as interested in women as another woman could be. These individuals come to assume the position of men who entertain homosexual rapport with women. Similarly, there are women who behave like male homosexuals. A woman of this species has no time for other women. What she likes is to be a boy among boys and she develops quasi-masculine homosexual relationships with men.

I think the magic moment occurs when a couple meet and intertwine in such a way that the hermaphroditism of both partners balances and integrates. It is the denial of this that lies at the origin of the sexual imbalances acted out physically, whether it is the more obvious polarisation into an exclusive homosexuality or whether homosexuality is, as it were, acted out within an apparently heterosexual relationship. When the man understands that he is also psychologically a woman, the woman can in turn recognise her masculine qualities.

Of course a woman can do violence to her femininity by striving to cultivate the masculine side of herself that competes with men, or at least by trying to survive in a masculine world in which it is necessary to adapt to these masculine traits in order to really compete. But this masculine constellation contains within itself a negation of the femininity of men. A vicious circle is thus created. To compete with a man who has denied his femininity, a woman must in turn deny her own. By drawing a diagram, it is easy to deduce schematically, on a formal level, all the main forms of distortion.

Thus, when a man completes a woman and a woman completes a man, they can both meet without having to repress or fear anything. They can become one. And that is Paradise, or at least one of the closest experiences to Paradise that I can imagine being possible.

DIALOGUE 10
Intellectual Work

Caretti: *Did you know Pasolini?*

Laing: I have never met him, but I know some of his films.

Caretti: *Well, Pier Paolo Pasolini contrasted the 'intellectual pirate' with the Gramscian organic intellectual, the one who is different with the one who is complicitly adapted to the dominant ideology. What do you think is the task of the intellectual?*

Laing: First of all, my perspective is very different from the one implied in the question. I start first of all with myself. It is true, however, that my intellect is engaged in the world. It has always been, and still is, no less than in the past. It is, to a very large extent, a commitment to theory. To engage in theory is to concentrate with our mind's eye and all our senses on trying to discern what patterns emerge and in particular what connections, more specifically those patterns that connect the different patterns we see in a more immediate sense. The ways in which we can use our minds are many, but it seems to me that the intellectual differs from other equally or more intelligent and cultured people, whether they be, for example, physicists or chemists or lawyers or politicians and so on, in the ways in which we use our minds. We commonly use the term 'intellectual' to designate one who says what he thinks about the way things are, who ponders carefully and puts forward such and such an idea or theory or proposal. Although the intellectual is socially engaged, being an activist is not among the essential traits of the intellectual (nor is not being an activist). However, it must be recognised that intellectual engagement in the world is a kind of praxis. We do not limit the concept of praxis to bodily movements in space. At different times in my life I might have asked myself "How do I use my mind?" and "How should I use my mind?". Well, this is an attitude that I have largely abandoned because, as Groddeck says, we may think we are ourselves living our life but in reality we are being lived by it.

Of course there is always a tension between these two positions. If we say "We are being lived", we shrug off all responsibility, thus opening the door to any possible dishonesty. If, on the other hand, we insist exclusively on the idea that "we live our own lives" and make it apply to others as well, then, in the words of Nietzsche, we risk thinking of man as free for the sole purpose of being able to judge and condemn man. From this point of view, it is an expedient, albeit a paradoxical one, aimed through the imposition of unconditional freedom of man at getting on his nerves, at making him abject, submissive and servile. Think of

Nietzsche's idea of the priestly function of intimidation and control of humanity. It is a trick, and the result is slavery.

The truth is that, on the one hand I am responsible for the way my mind operates, and on the other hand I am a creation of my own mind. The part of me that goes outside my mind is itself a component of my mind. I am convinced that my sense of identity, my 'I', is a product of the mind. I find it a useful hallucination. Or, let us say, it is a kind of ship thanks to which I can travel in mental space. In mental space I am perfectly well and I am happy to have a mental vehicle, to have my own place and so on. It is therefore above all a question of discovering as I come to live my life what my mind is preparing for tomorrow, of observing its impetus and intentions. It is a question of trying to understand the ground we stand on. Lately, for example, I have been reading all kinds of books, and I do not know why I did and do. And yet, as I read them, I have the distinct feeling that I am doing it for a purpose which will eventually become clear to me, perhaps in a couple of months. Last year I started reading sonnets. I do not know why on earth I did that, since I had no particular interest in sonnets. But shortly after I started reading them, I found myself writing them. I did not expect to and I did not intend to, yet I suddenly found myself writing sonnets. I had no idea what I was writing about either. It was a surprise; not a total surprise but certainly something I could not have anticipated. It was not part of a conscious plan. Sometimes my mind consciously formulates a plan and sticks to it, but then I get the impression that the plan unfolds on its own. It is a bit like children looking at traffic lights. They say "Green!" and the green light appears; they say "Red!" and the red light appears. You can convince yourself by deceiving yourself that the lights have appeared because you have named them.

The point is how our mind works, and also, I suppose, what purpose we give it, what use we plan to make of it. We have to keep both these aspects in mind. I think I can say very simply that there are two strengths of our mind. The first is the specific contribution which, against the background of the intention to serve the common cause, the intellect must make to the elucidation of truth and the unmasking of error, ignorance, lies, deception and mystification. It seems to me that the function of the intellect consists in this work of elucidating reality. The specific role of the intellectual in society is to use this capacity in the service of truth or the common good of the cosmos (and not necessarily in the service of that which immediately benefits the human race). This includes birds and bees, whales and also our entire egoic system, since the intellect should not be seen as a mere tool or instrument.

In fact, we do not use the intellect, and in this idea of 'used' is expressed a false conception of the nature of the intellect. It is not something like a screwdriver, nor is it like a telescope. It is not one of our instruments. Rather, the intellect is the builder of these instruments, which it has designed for its own purposes. The intellect is thus the exact opposite of an instrument. It is the creator of instruments. I mean this maker of instruments is not itself an instrument. The intellect can certainly use its own brain as an instrument, like a biological computer. But the brain is susceptible of many other uses, not unlike our hand, which we can use to caress or to slap, to manoeuvre a knife and fork or to play the most sublime music, or even to grab a dagger by the hasp when we kill someone. The brain exhibits the greatest diversification of functions. And the brain is not our intellect. In fact, the former uses the latter. To function, the intellect needs the brain, but I do not believe that the intellect is an epiphenomenon of the brain. Again we are faced with a dual figure: brain and intellect, the use we make of our intellect and the use our intellect makes of us. Taking up an old Platonic concept, it is important to emphasise the fact that the intellect is not only concerned with so-called 'truth' – cold, insensitive, heartless. The intellect is erotic. It is moved by eros, perhaps even by hatred. Let us say that the spiritual conflict or war between good and evil, love and hate, solicitude and indifference, union and separation, simmers in the intellect. So an intellect can be inclined either to evil or to good. It can commit itself to perpetuating hatred, malevolence, resentment and destruction, or to making our lives happier, more pleasant, decent and enjoyable for all creatures. It can rely on lies and falsehood. It can fall in love with deception but also with truth. Finally, I would say that the proper use of the intellect includes the ability or the art or the gift of transmitting and expressing our own life to other human beings. Besides being pure receptivity, the intellect in short is communication.

DIALOGUE 11
A Profession of Faith

Caretti: *William Blake, in his description of the divided states of being found in his prophetic books, notes a certain tendency to become what one perceives.* What have you perceived and what have you become after all these years of experience? Has there been a symbolic image that you have pursued or been guided by?

Laing: There are two images that seem to me to sum up what I have been searching for for so long. One is a multiplicity of different melodies or structures unfolding in reciprocal connection and alternating in the course of time with moments of discord, sometimes even constant discord, and moments of conflict resolution – in short, a temporal sequence of relationships between different trajectories that taken together make up a metastructure. Each of these threads, each melody is a temporal structure and a multiplicity of such structures forms a new structure, which connects the first ones, that is, the metastructure. In spatial terms they again represent the interweaving of different curves which intersect each other and flow freely in each direction, giving rise as we have seen to a metastructure. This offers me at least a glimpse, a sketch of a metaphor for the nature of my becoming. What I see is a structure of which I myself am a part. The structure I grasp as the metastructure that connects the structures I perceive is itself one of the structures in which and for which my seeing takes place.

Of course, there are many things I do not see. In other words, I do not see myself as an entity, or as an 'I-substance' or in the many other ways in which some people seem to look at themselves. But, after all, these allusions are the closest I can come to a description of myself as I see myself.

Caretti: *This brings us to the last question. In* The Politics of Experience *you said that the external separated from all illumination from the inner lives in darkness, and you concluded "Ours is an age of darkness". I have also often heard you quote Heidegger's sentence "The terrible has already happened". Perhaps you believe in Kali-Yuga*[34] *or do you think you have lost all hope?*

Laing: I find it very difficult to use the expression 'believe in'. After all, I am not able to say that I 'believe in' a certain thing without feeling that I have to explain this statement or qualify it. Similarly, there are those who find it very easy to say "I love you", but for me it is not an easy thing to say. I cannot say whether I 'believe' in Kali-Yuga or not. We are talking about great expanses of time, and a pattern of evolution and degradation of the cosmos that some men claim has been revealed to them. They do not say that they have imagined or constituted it but that they have entered into a state of Brahmanical consciousness. You can picture it by thinking of the view from a helicopter, which is enormously wider than that available to anyone on the ground. If you introduce time duration and contemplate it, you see that we are going round in circles and that a cosmic day-night rhythm is discernible in time over thousands of years. Well, if I had not heard about it, I would not have been able to compose this picture from my own experience. This experience, fragmentary as it may be, nevertheless tells me that it is not implausible, and especially in certain moods I feel it to be very congenial. But does this mean that I believe it? I would say no. I do not believe it, but neither am I convinced that it is not true.

In such a conceived time, I no longer know where we are, whether at the beginning or the end, whether our real story is just beginning, or whether our species is becoming extinct. I do not know if our ecosystem will be irreparably destroyed in the next twenty or thirty years, or if we are at an extreme point in the pendulum's swing and are therefore about to move in the opposite direction. This is often how change happens, by turning around and heading in the opposite direction. I do not know what the future holds for us and I do not see any pattern in the past that goes beyond what is historically documented. Palaeontologists tell us that as a species we appeared perhaps a million, perhaps two million, perhaps even six million years ago. God knows how far back our origins go. Then a biologist explains to me that biologists still believe in evolution but with virtually no proof. I hear that there is literally no evidence for gradualism; that is, for the evolution of a species after its appearance. In short, everything I was once taught about the evolutionary sequence of the human race is completely suspended in the void. As it turns out, the most remote fossils we have discovered are in every way similar to us. And the recent dating of these various skulls, etc. does not point to a linear transformation of that kind at all. On the other hand, so far every other species we have studied appears to us simply to have been be born, to last for a certain time, and then to die out.

A thousand, two thousand or three thousand years ago, the Earth may have had some reasonably pleasant moments from time to time, but history seems to consist largely of terrible massacres and torture, endless wars, slaughter, cruelty and enslavement. Certainly, I do not have the feeling that things are worse today. As far as I can see, the comparison is in some cases positive, in some others negative. Some repugnant things have disappeared, others no less repugnant have reappeared.

In fact, today I do not like that sentence of Heidegger's that you remembered, "The terrible has already happened". I do not know where I got it anymore and it might not even be Heidegger's. It might be a false memory. I am no longer as convinced as I used to be. I am not even sure what it means anymore. It is a sound sentence, the kind that always awakens echoes in me. It counts more for the effect it has than for its content. If I could hazard a guess as to its meaning, I would say that what we see in action in history often appears to be, so to speak, the echo in the external world of a state of affairs that has already taken place in the human soul. It is a sentence similar to that which says "God is dead" or to the Plutarchian sentence

"The great Pan is dead". Something has happened. A lament runs across the sea from the island, we read in Plutarch, and announces "The great Pan is dead".

I do not believe that if something has happened to the inner life, to the spiritual life of humanity (for example the total loss of the sense of the divine), the devastation and destruction of our ecosystem must necessarily follow. But it is true that we have lost a source of light. It is like the story of the two neighbours. One has a magnificent tree, whose branches extend over the roof of the other's house. The leaves settle on the eaves and every now and then they have to be brushed off. Well, why should we not cut down the damn tree? We live in a world where we are constantly cutting down trees, even in a literal sense. Think of the forests that end up in newsprint every day or in the paper used to make my books, and so on. This could be the external manifestation (i.e. an echo) of this 'terrible' that has already happened. Even deeper abysses have been foretold or prophetically announced. I am thinking of Nietzsche's "God is dead." He adds that there are idiots dancing and clapping their hands and partying.

On the whole, we have managed to maintain a certain balance between good and bad things. The Europe of 1978 is definitely not the worst place that has ever appeared on the scene of history, although the worst things that have happened in the past can still happen. I would much rather live in present-day London than in Flaubert's Carthage. At the height of Greek civilisation, the condition of the intellectual must have been very uncomfortable if Socrates' fate could have been the death sentence.

Nor in those days could an intellectual do more (though perhaps he did it more effectively) than an enlightened modern intellectual can today. To educate does not mean to inspire in people answers to questions they have never even asked, but rather to pose the question and then like a midwife draw out of the educated one the answer (if there is an answer at all).

In conclusion, I am not obsessed with the historical fantasy that things will go from bad to worse. But I do feel that we are walking on the razor's edge. By using technology in an unhinged, ruthless and instrumental way, we are destroying our ecosystem. Or at least that is the idea I have from what I have read and heard. The ecologists I have met are generally well-balanced people and they do not seem to have apocalyptic end-of-the-world fantasies. Yet, without even raising their voices, they keep saying that we are rapidly destroying the system that sustains our life and that at this rate the process may soon become irreversible. I do not believe that this is inevitable. I have not lost a sense of hope and faith. I remember Camus used to say "Enough with the dirty hopes". Of course many, many hopes are illusions. But I understand hope in its authentic sense. Hope in its true sense concerns the possible, not the impossible. A hope aimed at the impossible which nevertheless wants to persist is an illusion. It is not possible for the human race to be immortal, any more than any one of us can be immortal in our individuality. It seems to me that the human race is an animal species and we have every reason to suppose that, like all other animal species, it is destined for a limited life span. How close are we to the end? Are we experiencing the conclusion of the story? Or are we still in the middle? Or maybe in the first act? And how will it end? Who knows? What is certain is that the story will have an ending. There will come a time when on the face of this planet, in this cosmos, the last human being, whether man or woman, will draw his or her last breath. After that, there will be nothing left but a pile of bones and after that no trace of us, and therefore no human universe as we know it – no images, no sounds, no smells, no tastes as we know them. All these things cannot exist without human brains and we have no idea what will be in the future. Whether it is a benign or horrible process (according to the categories of our feeble minds) I cannot say, but I have faith and hope. Regarding what we know, we need neither hope nor faith. As for what lies beyond, I know that at certain times I hope and at others I despair. I hope on Mondays, Thursdays and Sundays, and despair on Tuesdays and Saturdays, and sometimes I have faith, sometimes not. But I have certainly lost neither hope nor faith.

Endnotes

1. Laing, R. D. (1960). *The Divided Self: An existential study in sanity and madness*. Harmondsworth: Penguin
2. *Satipatthana*, 'The Establishment of Mindfulness' or 'Foundations of Mindfulness', is a Pali Buddhist text (*Satipatthana Sutta*) on Vipassana meditation. For a translation of the *Satipatthana Sutta*, see Soma, B. (trans. and ed.) (1949). *The Way of Mindfulness*. Colombo: Lake House.
3. *Vipassana*, 'Conscious Vision [In-Sight]', is a particular type of meditation based on global attention to everything that presents itself to consciousness. It also refers to the moments of insight that can occur during meditation.
4. *Anapanasati*, 'Mindfulness of Breathing', is a special type of meditation based on the relevant section of the *Satipatthana Sutta* and consists of following the natural course of breathing. An alternative method of practice, which starts with counting the breaths, is described in the *Visuddhimagga*.
5. Laing, R. D. (1976). *The Facts of Life*. London: Penguin.
6. McCulloch, W.S. (1965). What the frog's eye tells the frog's brain. In *Embodiments of Mind*. Cambridge: MIT Press. 230.
7. Bacon, F. (1620). The great instauration. In Robertson, J.M. (ed.) (1905). *The Philosophical Works of Francis Bacon*. London: Routledge. 252.
8. According to the *Tibetan Book of the Dead* (*Bardo Thodol*), at the moment of death, when the body is disposed of and the breath ceases, one enters the state of intermediate existence (*bardo*) in which either salvation or rebirth ripens.
9. Popper, K.R. & Eccles, J.C. (1977). *The Self and Its Brain*. New York: Springer.
10. Huxley, T.H. (1874). On the hypothesis that animals are automata. Quoted in Popper and Eccles, op. cit. 72.
11. Mitchell, J. (1974). *Psychoanalysis And Feminism*. New York: Basic Books. 273.
12. Shakespeare, W. *Macbeth*. Act II, Scene i. 33-34.
13. Dhoti is a fabric, usually white in colour, which Indians wear rolled around the waist as a garment.
14. Laing, R.D. & Cooper, D.G. (1964). *Reason and Violence: A century of Sartre's philosophy*. London: Tavistock.
15. Laing, R.D. (1971). *The Politics of the Family and Other Essays*. London: Tavistock.
16. Laing, R.D. (1967). *The Politics of Experience*. New York: Pantheon. 53.
17. Fromm, E., Suzuki, D. & Martino, R. de (1960). *Zen Buddhism and Psychoanalysis*. New York: Haper and Row.
18. Zendo is the room or environment where Zazen meditation is practised.

19. *Koan* is a technical term in Zen Buddhism. It means a problem that cannot be solved by the intellect. It is also understood as an exercise that serves to break down the barriers of the intellect and develop intuition.
20. Deleuze, G. & Guattari, F. (1977). *Anti-Oedipus: Capitalism and schizophrenia*. Minneapolis: University of Minnesota Press.
21. Laing, R.D. (1971). The family and the 'family'. In *The Politics of the Family*. op. cit. 15.
22. Barnes, M. & Berke, J. (1971). *Two Accounts of a Journey through Madness*. London: MacGibbon and Kee.
23. Laing, R.D. (1966). Ritualization and abnormal behaviour. In *Philosophical Transactions of the Royal Society of London*. 251: 772. 29 December. 331-335.
24. *Visuddhimagga*, 'The Path of Purification', is a text from the late exegetical literature of Pali Buddhism. For a translation of the *Visuddhimagga*, see Ñanamoli, B, (trans. and ed.) (1956). *The Path of Purification*. Colombo: Semage.
25. Grof, S. (1975). *Realms of the Human Unconscious*. New York: Viking.
26. Lilly, J. (1972). *The Center of the Cyclone*. New York: Julian Press.
27. Naranjo, C. (1973). *The Healing Journey*. New York: Pantheon Books.
28. Lake, F. (1966). *Clinical Theology: A theological and psychiatric basis to clinical pastoral care*. London: Darton.
29. Birdwhistell, R.L. (1973). *Kinesics and Context: Essays on body-motion communication*. Harmondsworth: Penguin Books.
30. Fromm, E. (1951). *The Forgotten Language: An introduction to the understanding of dreams, fairy tales and myths*. New York: Rinehart & Company.
31. Wittgenstein, L. (1998). *Tractatus Logico-Philosophicus*. London: Routledge. 4.1212 [*"Was gezeigt werden kann, kann nicht gesagt werden"*].
32. Laing, R.D. (1976). *The Facts of Life*. op. cit. 149.
33. Laing, R.D. (1967). *The Politics of Experience* and *The Bird of Paradise*. London: Penguin.
34. Kali Yuga is the last of the four ages (yuga) in Indian tradition. Kali Yuga, which corresponds to our era, is considered to be "the age of darkness".

ALSO AVAILABLE IN THE DIALOGUE SERIES

Dialogues on the Search for Meaning in Existential Therapy
Ernesto Spinelli and Gianfranco Buffardi
Available on Amazon

Dialogues on the Soul of Existential Therapy
Professor Miles Groth and Professor Todd DuBose
Available on Amazon

Dialogues on the Renaissance of Daseinanalysis
Professor Miles Groth and Professor Tamás Fazekas
Available on Amazon

ACKNOWLEDGEMENTS
Many thanks to:
Dean Andrews for typesetting and formatting the manuscript
Adam Knowles for the online printing process

All proceeds from sales of this publication have been kindly donated to the SEA.

SEA
The Society for Existential Analysis

The Society for Existential Analysis is a Registered Charity no.1039274, whose objectives are, among others,

"... to raise awareness of the value of the Existential approach to philosophical, ethical and social issues possibly by providing speakers, publications and occasions of public meetings and courses, including different modalities and subjects complementary to psychotherapy, such as philosophy or psychology."

www.existentialanalysis.org.uk

Made in the USA
Las Vegas, NV
15 March 2025